THE
TRANSCENDENTALIST REVOLT
AGAINST MATERIALISM

Problems in American Civilization

PREPARED UNDER THE EDITORSHIP OF

Earl Latham
George Rogers Taylor
George F. Whicher

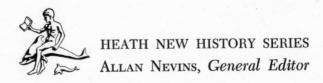

HEATH NEW HISTORY SERIES
ALLAN NEVINS, *General Editor*

The Transcendentalist
Revolt against
Materialism

EDITED WITH AN INTRODUCTION BY

George F. Whicher

Problems in American Civilization

READINGS SELECTED BY THE
DEPARTMENT OF AMERICAN STUDIES
AMHERST COLLEGE

D. C. HEATH AND COMPANY: Boston

Offices

Boston   New York   Chicago   Dallas
Atlanta   San Francisco   London

INTRODUCTION

UNTIL very recently the American tendency has been to regard government as a necessary evil, to be kept as near a minimal level as possible. An influential section of the people has always disliked official interference. Extensive programs of social legislation have been fiercely resented. The motives of political leaders have been distrusted, even when they were honestly working for the public welfare. The best men, it is often said, simply will not go into politics. But perhaps the welfare state is now with us to stay and a good citizen can no longer afford to neglect his political duties. The issue raised by the readings chosen for this volume is whether a man eager to improve the quality of American life can work most effectually through political channels or by some other means. The problem is a perennial one, which vexed men in the age of Pericles as well as in the days of Andrew Jackson.

About 1836 and for a few years thereafter a group of young New England intellectuals fell into a way of meeting together in Concord, Massachusetts, to discuss new developments in philosophy, theology, and literature. They were greatly stimulated by the exciting ideas originated by German thinkers and circulated among English-speaking readers in the writings of Coleridge, Wordsworth, and Carlyle.

Generally the group met in the study of Ralph Waldo Emerson, a former Uni-

tarian minister who had left his pulpit in order that he might be free to think and write his own unfettered thoughts. It included other youthful and earnest clergymen such as Theodore Parker of West Roxbury, George Ripley of Boston, and F. H. Hedge of Bangor, but among the members were also numbered the progressive schoolteacher and philosopher Amos Bronson Alcott, the poets W. E. Channing and Jones Very, and a recent graduate of Harvard named Henry Thoreau. Thoughtful women were represented by Mrs. Ripley, Elizabeth Peabody, and Margaret Fuller. The novelist Nathaniel Hawthorne, the journalist Orestes W. Brownson, and several now forgotten figures sometimes attended the highly informal meetings.

The neighbors in fun christened the gathering the Transcendental Club, borrowing what may have seemed an uncouth term from the philosophy of Immanuel Kant. The name, however, stuck, and has since become an accepted label for the New England idealists of this period.

The transcendentalists were deeply concerned about the quality of life in America. A great tide of material prosperity, checked only temporarily by the crises of 1837 and 1839 and the ensuing depression, had overtaken the country. Everything was expanding by leaps and bounds. Virgin territories were being opened to settlement from Illinois to Oregon. Turnpikes, canals, steamboats, railroads were rushed into being. The fur trade, overseas commerce, whaling, the cotton culture of the South, the factories of the North were bringing wealth to a happy nation. It was an era of good feeling, a time when the common man seemed to be getting his share of creature comforts. Yet sensitive observers feared that all was not well. It appeared not unlikely that care for man's intellectual and spiritual nature might be submerged in the rush for easy riches. What would be the profit in all this material advance if it were not matched by an equal progress in humanity? So the transcendentalists pondered.

Traditionally the church had attended to the spiritual well-being of the community. The original colonists of Massachusetts Bay had hoped to found "Christ's kingdom in the wilderness." They were energized by the sense of a God-given mission and held to their purpose by a rigid Calvinistic creed. But in the course of the eighteenth century the early zeal had cooled, worldly concerns came crowding in to lessen religious dedication, and rationalistic thinking sapped the Puritan creed. What remained then was a formal institution, the Unitarian church, decorous, tolerant, and reasonable. It had no burning convictions to prevent men from laying waste their powers in getting and spending. "Corpse-cold," Emerson called it; a religion of pale negations, satisfactory to Boston merchants and Harvard professors, but not to those who still cherished the ancient fire of Puritan mysticism or sought to realize the New World dream of a regenerate humanity. And among these were Emerson and his friends.

They did not approve of the low commercial tone of Boston. Human nature, they held, possessed infinite possibilities of development. Man was not meant for money-grubbing. His moral being demanded a larger share of attention than it was receiving. But how could a change of heart be effected? Certainly not through politics, that sordid arena where the Jacksonian mob and the slightly more respectable Whigs squabbled in dust and heat. Would it not be better to appeal in a dignified way to man's moral nature by means of pulpit, school, and press? Or if a reform of institutions were in question, why not proceed at once to the realization, even in a small way, of an ideally cooperative society? Questions like these occupied the transcendental group.

In systematic terms the contrast between "the philosophy of sensationalism" (materialism) and "the philosophy of transcendentalism" was elaborated by Theodore Parker, whose interpretative essay on "Transcendentalism" (1876) has been recognized by recent scholarship as one of the best contemporary accounts of the movement. Readers who wish to obtain a vivid sense of what evils a transcendental clergyman was assailing and what opposition he was encountering cannot do better than to consult the white-hot testament which he composed as a letter to his congregation and published under the title of *Theodore Parker's Experiences as a Minister* (1859). This moving document is too long to be quoted here, but the excerpts from Professor Commager's life of Parker will indicate that he served a sufficiently useful function, not by participating directly in politics, but by making himself through contacts with his political friends "the Conscience of a Party."

When Emerson, in a lecture delivered in 1842, undertook to characterize "The Transcendentalist," he associated the idealism practiced by his representative

INTRODUCTION vii

modern thinker with the intransigent attitudes of Stoics and Covenanters and other strong spirits down the ages:

This way of thinking, falling on Roman times, made Stoic philosophers; falling on despotic times, made patriot Catos and Brutuses; falling on superstitious times, made prophets and apostles; on popish times, made protestants and ascetic monks, preachers of Faith against preachers of Works; on prelatical times, made Puritans and Quakers; and falling on Unitarian and commercial times, makes the peculiar shades of Idealism which we know.

The clerical background and training of the transcendentalists predisposed them to think of stimulating men's minds and consciences by a religious revival such as the Great Awakening that had swept New England a century before. Their strategy was to strike directly at motives, to control men by capturing their imaginations, enlisting their wills, and rousing them to an outpouring of faith. They had slight respect for gradual measures. Society in their view was not something to be continuously molded, but to be abruptly fixed once for all.

Practical politicians, however, do not expect to work by regenerating their constituents. They labor diligently to organize individuals and groups as they find them into parties which in turn may be capable of establishing specific acts and institutions of government. "We the people" place in office the party of our election. Our government is made in our own image. If we are not well governed, we have no one but ourselves to blame. The system is far short of perfection, but after a fashion it works.

At the period we are discussing the two major parties were the Whigs and the Democrats. The former, led by Henry Clay and Daniel Webster, were the inheritors of Alexander Hamilton's political philosophy. They tried by all means to promote commerce and manufactures, and to secure the ascendancy of the moneyed interests, on the theory that if merchants and mill-owners were prospering the country at large would share in their prosperity. They were the party of respectability and the status quo.

Opposed to them were the somewhat nondescript partisans who followed the leadership of Andrew Jackson and his successors. They were Jeffersonian without the patrician touch. To many they seemed a dangerous rabble. But they were clearly a people's party, committed to extending the franchise, favoring the small farmer rather than the speculator in their land legislation, jealous of concentration of financial power in the hands of a few, and determined to make of the national government an effective instrument to protect the wage-earner from exploitation.

As Professor Schlesinger demonstrates in the chapter from *The Age of Jackson* quoted in the selections that follow, the program of the Democrats appealed to a large number of contemporary intellectuals and literary men. Bancroft and Paulding held cabinet posts under Democratic administrations, Whitman and O'Sullivan were active political journalists, and even the retiring Hawthorne was willing to accept political appointments in the customs service, and later as U. S. consul, and to write a campaign biography in support of his friend Franklin Pierce. Only the transcendentalists for the most part, though theoretically in sympathy with the aims of the Democrats, remained aloof.

Emerson freely admitted the claims of the Democratic party to his allegiance. "The philosopher, the poet, or the religious man," he wrote, "will, of course, wish to cast his vote with the democrat, for free trade, for wide suffrage, for the abolition of legal cruelties in the penal code, and for facilitating in every manner the access of the young and the poor to the sources of wealth and power." Elsewhere in a moment of prophetic insight he declared that the mission of "this rank rabble party, the Jacksonism of the country," might be to establish a national culture on a soundly realistic basis, to "root out the hollow dilettantism of our cultivation in the coarsest way, and the newborn may begin again to frame their own world with greater advantage." But having paid lip-service to the policies of the Jacksonians, Emerson declined to take an active part in the hurlyburly of party politics. Did he thereby, as Professor Schlesinger intimates, fail in his obligations as a citizen of the republic and vitiate his own moral position?

When he was asked by his good friend W. H. Channing, an earnest social reformer, to support the crusade for the abolition of slavery, Emerson replied that he had other slaves to free, slaves to ignorance, superstition, and fear, and though he made his position on the slavery question clear on numerous occasions, he would not devote his entire energy to the promotion of any single reform, however important.

In their relation to politics the transcendentalists were confronted by a double question: they had to decide, first, whether they would try to make the world better by working to renovate man's nature or by organizing to improve his institutions; and second, if they chose the latter course, whether to attempt a gradual amelioration or a drastic and sudden change. Emerson and Thoreau consistently chose the moral rather than the political approach. Thoreau was capable of taking direct political action, as when he refused to pay his poll tax to a state implicated in the waging of an unjust war, or when he rose to the defense of John Brown's integrity of character after the raid on Harper's Ferry; but ordinarily he asked only that men should refrain from "pawing him with their dirty institutions." George Ripley when he launched the utopian adventure at Brook Farm, and Alcott when he plunged into the uncertainties of the Fruitlands project, were choosing the second alternative and were training to achieve at once a model of a perfect society without waiting for the slow process of social evolution.

These experiments in ideal living though both ended in practical failure, were not altogether futile. The community at Brook Farm, in particular, attracted wide attention and insistently raised the question of whether man's social adjustments might not be drastically improved. Even the short-lived Fruitlands venture, with all its fantastic and amusing extravagances, testified to the burning sincerity with which some men devoted themselves and their families to visionary schemes for the betterment of the human race. A highly successful school was conducted at Brook Farm, while the philosophers at Fruitlands assembled the largest collection of Oriental literature then available in the United States.

We return to the question at issue. Were Emerson and his friends misguided in refraining from politics and making their appeal directly to the hearts of men? Could Ripley and Alcott have served the country better if like Hawthorne they had given a stanch allegiance to party and accepted political duties and rewards?

James Truslow Adams, the distinguished historian, has in a general way questioned the maturity of Emerson's outlook:

If . . . we find his culture a bit thin and puerile, is it not because he himself trusted too much to that spirit of spontaneity, of the "spontaneous glance," rather than to the harder process of scholarship and thinking-through coherently; and if we find him lacking in depth and virility, is it not because he allowed himself to become a victim to that vast American optimism with its refusal to recognize and wrestle with the problem of evil?

On the other hand, Professor R. H. Gabriel of Yale, another highly competent student of social history, credits Emerson with an important service to the American culture of his time:

Emerson impressed the common folk of his generation because he preached a philosophy of individualism that not only seemed to set men free, but to provide them with dynamic, creative energy. He gave the doctrine of the free individual sharpness of definition, causing it to emerge, with the clarity of an etching, from the cloudy background of half-formulated ideas.

Thus Emerson with his transcendental associates may be pictured as an ineffective and fastidious perfectionist. Or he may be described as a fountainhead of dynamic currents that set men's creative powers in motion. Which is the truer estimate of what Browning calls "the man's amount"?

Now who shall arbitrate?
Ten men love what I hate,
Shun what I follow, slight what I receive. . . .

But differences of interpretation are the stuff out of which valid judgments are molded. Each of us is entitled to forge and wield an opinion of his own.

CONTENTS

The Clash of Issues

"Our citizens attend both to public and private duties, and do not allow absorption in their own various affairs to interfere with their knowledge of the city's. We differ from other states in regarding the man who holds aloof from public life not as 'quiet' but as useless."

—THUCYDIDES: *The Funeral Oration of Pericles*

"This is what deters me from being a politician. And rightly, as I think. For I am certain, O men of Athens, that if I had engaged in politics, I should have perished long ago, and done no good either to you or to myself. . . . He who will fight for the right, if he would live even for a brief space, must have a private station and not a public one."

—PLATO: *The Apology of Socrates*

"I have not yet conquered my own house. It irks and repents me. Shall I raise the siege of this hencoop, and march baffled away to a pretended siege of Babylon? It seems to me that so to do were to dodge the problem I am set to solve, and to hide my impotency in the thick of a crowd."

—RALPH WALDO EMERSON: *Journals,* October 17, 1840

"For the typical transcendentalist the flinching from politics perhaps expressed a failure they were seeking to erect into a virtue. The exigencies of responsibility were exhausting: much better to demand perfection and indignantly reject the half loaf, than wear out body and spirit in vain grapplings with overmastering reality."

—ARTHUR M. SCHLESINGER, JR.: *The Age of Jackson*

Arthur M. Schlesinger, Jr.:
JACKSONIAN DEMOCRACY AND LITERATURE

1

HISTORIANS of revolution describe a phenomenon they have named the "desertion of the intellectuals." This is the stage in society when the artists, the writers, the intellectuals in general, no longer find enough sustenance in the established order to feel much loyalty to it. They are filled with a pervading sense at once of alienation and of longing, which, one way or another, controls their work, directly if they are political writers, obliquely and at many removes if they are poets. The age of Jackson was such a period. One world was passing away, while another struggled to be born, and the political battles of the Jacksonians helped set in motion a whole train of changes in other spheres. "The strife has been of a character to call forth all the resources of the popular intelligence," Theodore Sedgwick, Jr., wrote in 1835, ". . . It has urged forward the whole American mind."[1]

Not all writers were politically active, not even all those possessed by visions of a new world. Some, like Emerson and Thoreau, preoccupied most profoundly with the questions raised up by the change, spent years quietly ignoring politics. But, even with such important exceptions, it is yet remarkable how many of the leading authors and artists publicly aligned themselves with the Jacksonian party. Nathaniel Hawthorne, William Cullen Bryant, Walt Whitman, James Fenimore Cooper, George Bancroft, Washington Irving (until the pressure became too great), James K. Paulding, Orestes A. Brownson, William Leggett, John L. O'Sullivan, John L. Stephens, Horatio Greenough, Hiram Powers, Edwin Forrest, Frances Wright, Robert Dale Owen, for example, were all Jacksonians. As Harriet Martineau observed, the Democratic party included the underprivileged classes, the careerists, the humanitarians and "an accession small in number, but inestimable in power, — the men of genius."[2]

[1] Sedgwick, *What Is a Monopoly?*, 7. It would require another and a different book to show how the literature of the day tried to resolve on the moral and artistic level some of the problems faced by Jacksonian democracy in politics and economics. Much of this ground has been acutely covered by F. O. Matthiessen in *American Renaissance*. My purpose here is simply to indicate some of the direct responses of writers to politics.

[2] Martineau, *Society in America*, I, 13–14. Cf. George Combe, *Notes on the United States of North America*, II, 216: "The Whig party in America claims the wealth of the Union on their side, and the Democrats claim the genius."

The Democrats were exceedingly proud of their intellectuals. "It is a fact well known," boasted the *Boston Post*, "that with few exceptions, our first literary men belong to the democratic party. Almost every man of note in letters, — historians, poets, and indeed nearly all who have acquired fame as writers and authors are, as might be expected, favorable to democracy."[3] Van Buren himself offered government jobs to Bancroft, Hawthorne, Irving, Paulding, Brownson and Leggett. Even Whigs complained that the word "Locofoco" ought to be used as the "synonyme of ignorance; and yet that party certainly numbers amongst its leaders some celebrated literary characters."[4] For many this fact was cause for indignation. "Why in this fearful struggle which we are obliged to sustain," cried Edward Everett of Hawthorne, "is he on the side of barbarism & vandalism against order, law & constitutional liberty?"[5]

Many of the authors regarded a position of political liberalism as an artistic imperative. They felt that the Whigs cared only to preserve the tame, reliable and derivative culture of which men like Everett and Longfellow were faithful representatives. The only future for a powerful native literature, dealing fearlessly in truth and reality, seemed to lie in a bold exploration of the possibilities of democracy. "The vital principle of an American national literature," declared the *Democratic Review*, "must be democ-

racy."[6] "The man of letters," as George Bancroft told Everett, "should be the man of the people," and his own monumental *History* revealed how a living faith in the people could quicken, unify and transmute into art a narrative which had heretofore been but dry chronicles.[7] Orestes A. Brownson was even more specific. The question of capital and labor seemed to him supreme: "In the struggle of these two elements, true American literature will be born."[8]

2

A first requisite for a literature is a medium for publication. The respectable magazines — the *North American,* the *American Quarterly,* the *New-England Magazine,* and so on — were in Whig hands, and during the eighteen-thirties the need for a monthly journal of liberal sympathies became increasingly pronounced. At this juncture a bright young man named John L. O'Sullivan, who had been running a small newspaper in Washington, appeared with the project of a Democratic review.

O'Sullivan was descended from a long line of picaresque Irishmen whose actual careers remain buried under family legend. His father had lived an obscure life, sometimes as American Consul in such places as Mogador and Teneriffe,

---

[3] *Boston Post,* October 11, 1838. See also *New York Evening Post,* August 14, 1838.

[4] Francis Baylies, *Speech . . . before the Whigs of Taunton,* 3.

[5] Everett to G. S. Hillard, June 21, 1849, Everett Papers. Henry Wadsworth Longfellow charged darkly in 1839 that the Locofocos were organizing a "new politico-literary system." Longfellow to G. W. Greene, July 23, 1839, Hawthorne, *The American Notebooks,* Randall Stewart, ed., 288.

[6] "Introduction," *Democratic Review,* I, 14 (October, 1837).

[7] Bancroft to Everett, February 7, 1835, Bancroft Papers. Cf. Bancroft to Jared Sparks, August 22, 1834, Sparks Papers: "A vein of public feeling, of democratic independence, of popular liberty, ought to be infused into our literature. Let Mammon rule in the marts, but not on the holy mountain of letters. The rich ought not to be flattered; let truth, let humanity speak through the public journals and through American literature."

[8] Brownson, "American Literature," *Boston Quarterly Review,* III, 76 (January, 1840).

more often as master, supercargo or owner of ships engaged in the South American trade. A cloud of mystery hangs over many of his transactions, and he was several times charged with bribery and extortion and even suspected of piracy. One aunt paid a call on ex-President Madison in 1827, dressed as a man and followed by four children, and told a fantastic tale of adventures in Europe and America.[9]

Young O'Sullivan graduated from Columbia in 1831 and began a life of free-lance journalism. He was a charming, gay and rather indolent man, with a sanguine temperament, often disappointed but rarely depressed. Nathaniel Hawthorne, while feeling him to be superficial, very much enjoyed his company, and a sterner nature like Thoreau thought him "puny-looking" and over-talkative but still one of the "not-bad." O'Sullivan's sister (handsome enough to provoke even Emerson to enthusiastic comment) had married another young writer named S. D. Langtree, and together in 1837 the two approached Benjamin F. Butler with the proposal of a Democratic literary magazine.[10]

Butler, who was given to cultural dabbling and even wrote verse for publication, took fire at the idea, subscribed five hundred dollars himself and urged other Democratic politicians to aid in financing the *Democratic Review*. Henry D. Gilpin also took an active part in the search for backing. Jackson, who had long hoped for such a journal, encouraged the project and became the first subscriber. During the summer the editors approached writers the country over, and in October a preliminary number appeared, with contributions by Bryant, Hawthorne, Whittier and others. (When Langtree applied to John Quincy Adams, the old man testily replied that literature by its nature would always be aristocratic, and that the idea of a Democratic literary magazine was self-contradictory.)[11]

Whatever O'Sullivan's failings, he was an excellent editor. He was assiduous in seeking out new talent, and he quickly made the *Democratic Review* by far the liveliest journal of the day. His authors included Bryant, Hawthorne, Thoreau, Whittier, Walt Whitman, Poe, Longfellow, Lowell, Paulding, William Gilmore Simms, Bancroft, Brownson, A. H. Everett and many more. Politically the magazine aligned itself vigorously with the radical wing of the party. The *Madisonian* described it as a "sort of political hygroscope, indicating the state of the air breathed in the party councils of the ruling dynasty," and even men like

[9] J. W. Pratt, "John L. O'Sullivan and Manifest Destiny," *New York History*, XXXI, 214–217.

[10] Poe thought him an ass, and Longfellow, a humbug — both judgments occasionally having their foundation. Julia Ward Howe, meeting Yeats, in 1903, and noting his fiery temperament, his slight figure, his blue eyes and dark hair, was irresistibly reminded of O'Sullivan. Julian Hawthorne, *Nathaniel Hawthorne and His Wife*, I, 160; Nathaniel Hawthorne, *Love Letters*, Roswell Field, ed., II, 242; Rose H. Lathrop, *Memories of Hawthorne*, 77; Thoreau to Emerson, January 24, 1843, F. B. Sanborn, *Hawthorne and His Friends*, 30; G. E. Woodberry, *Life of Edgar Allan Poe*, I, 353; Hawthorne, *The American Notebooks*, 288–289; Laura E. Richards and Maud Howe Elliott, *Julia Ward Howe, 1819–1910*, II, 319; Emerson to Margaret Fuller, February 24, 1843, Emerson, *Letters*, III, 149.

[11] O'Sullivan to Rufus Griswold, September 8, 1842, *Passages from the Correspondence of Rufus W. Griswold*, William Griswold, ed., 213; Butler to Bancroft, May 1, 1838, Bancroft Papers; Butler to Gilpin, April 24, 1838, Gilpin Papers; Jackson to Langtree and O'Sullivan, March 6, 1837, *Washington Globe*, March 13, 1837; Adams, *Memoirs*, IX, 416; Frank L. Mott, *History of American Magazines*, I, 677–684.

Marcy regarded it as an "organ of the administration."[12] There is no evidence, however, that Van Buren used the *Democratic Review* for trial balloons, and in the end the magazine left Washington when Blair's jealousy denied it a share of the government printing.[13] It resumed publication in New York and remained under O'Sullivan's control till 1846. Its circulation in 1843 was 3500.[14]

In the meantime Orestes Brownson had provided the liberals with another organ in his *Boston Quarterly Review*. The concurrence of motives behind this

journal showed the wide front of the cultural revolt. His object, Brownson said, was to support the new movement in all its manifestations, "whether it be effecting a reform in the Church, giving us a purer and more rational theology; in philosophy seeking something profounder and more inspiriting than the heartless Sensualism of the last century; or whether in society demanding the elevation of labor with the Locofoco, or the freedom of the slave with the Abolitionist."[15]

The *Boston Quarterly* thus became a compendium of the desertion of the intellectuals, defending in detail the repudiation of the old order in religion, philosophy and politics. Not only Bancroft and A. H. Everett but George Ripley and Theodore Parker, Bronson Alcott and Margaret Fuller were essential in Brownson's broad purpose. To him the fight was all one, though later the political motive grew more dominant, and it almost seemed, as Brownson told Van Buren, that the review was established "for the purpose of enlisting Literature, Religion, and Philosophy on the side of Democracy."[16]

Less bright and varied than the *Democratic Review*, the *Boston Quarterly* was more learned, serious and penetrating. Brownson's personality pervaded the Journal — he became increasingly the exclusive author — and he endowed it with a vigor and cogency which commanded wide attention. John C. Calhoun, for example, was a faithful reader, and even the impassive Levi Woodbury, Secretary of the Treasury, was moved to exclaim of one issue, "What an excellent number was Mr. Brownson's last! Exhort him

[12] This reputation discredited the *Democratic Review* in conservative circles. "Will you believe," wrote George Sumner, from Europe, to a friend in Boston, "that because that article on Greece appeared in the *Democratic Review*, the only review we have which goes to foreign capitals, the review which champions in a moderate way those principles upon which our Government is founded, . . . the review which Advaros (Min. of Pub. Ins. in Russ.) hailed as a publication which gave a tone to America abroad, and enabled her to appear with a review not a poor repetition of the poor matter of the English reviews — because that article appeared in the *Democratic Review*, it is trodden under foot, and I am denounced as 'an Administration man.'" His brother Charles had written him that Nathan Hale refused to reprint the article in the *Boston Advertiser*; George Ticknor was "sorry to see it in such company"; Justice Story was "much troubled," but "of course did not speak of it out of delicacy to me"; Professor Greenleaf of the Harvard Law School was "grieved" and reported that it had been "lamented by many people who were prepared to be your friends." "Seriously, my dear George," Charles Sumner wrote, "think of abandoning your leaky craft." George Sumner's response was violent: "God *damn* them *all!!* . . . I cannot but laugh, roars of horrid laughter, on thinking of all these things. . . . How the demon of party feeling must have crazed the minds and feelings of men whose characters one would suppose firm and high." George Sumner to G. W. Greene, November [?], 1842, *Proceedings of the Massachusetts Historical Society*, XLVI, 359–360.

[13] Mott, *History of American Magazines*, I, 679–680.

[14] O'Sullivan to Charles Sumner, April 12, 1843, Sumner Papers.

[15] "Introductory Remarks," *Boston Quarterly Review*, I, 6 (January, 1838).

[16] Brownson to Van Buren, April 2, 1838, Van Buren Papers.

from me to give us more."[17] (When Brownson began a few months later to give them more, Woodbury became markedly less enthusiastic.)

In 1842 the *Democratic Review* and the *Boston Quarterly* merged, but not before each had left a distinct mark on the development of American letters. Each journal, on its own level, was the best of its day, and both gained much of their energy, courage and free vigor from their immersion in the political ideals of Jacksonian democracy.

3

A surprising number of writers were themselves active in politics or the government service. George Bancroft, driven ahead by an unstable combination of democratic idealism and personal ambition, became party boss of Massachusetts and later Polk's Secretary of the Navy. Brownson held office under Van Buren and ran for Congress during the Civil War. Washington Irving and Alexander H. Everett were in the diplomatic service.

James K. Paulding spent many years on government pay rolls, first as Naval Agent of New York, later as Van Buren's Secretary of the Navy. This bluff, amusing Dutchman was a stout Jacksonian, if by a roundabout road. A man of obstinate good sense, he disliked the cant of radicalism, but disliked the cant of conservatism even more. His famous satire *The Merry Tales of the Three Wise Men of Gotham* (1826) poked fun impartially at the common law, on the one hand, and the dreams of Robert Owen, on the other. Many brief political essays, bearing the stamp of his gruff irony and hearty common sense, appeared in the *Washington Globe* and the *New York Evening Post*.[18]

Nathaniel Hawthorne was another Democratic pensioner, holding office under three administrations. Unlike Paulding, he was not much of a party journalist, though there was once a possibility of his joining the *Globe* under Frank Blair, and in 1852 he wrote a campaign life of Franklin Pierce.[19] Yet he was not as perfunctory a Democrat as some biographers have insisted. His quiet sense of sin and his hatred of human pride immunized him against the claims of Whig conservatism to moral or political superiority. He was not much impressed by Utopianism either. The current of his sympathies, as expressed in his notebook jottings, ran clear and strong with the plain, solid, common life of the people. *The House of the Seven Gables* embodied massively his conviction of the fatal isolation worked by property and privilege, and his fascination with the rude energies of change and reform.[20] The "Locofoco Surveyor," as he described himself in the preface to *The Scarlet Letter*, was permanently marked by that day in 1833 when he walked through the falling shadows of a Salem dusk to catch a glimpse of General Andrew Jackson.

Of all the literary men of the day, however, James Fenimore Cooper has probably suffered the most inquiry into his politics. Because these examinations have generally been carried on without detailed knowledge of the concrete party

---

[17] Woodbury to Bancroft, November 21, 1839, Bancroft Papers.

[18] See Paulding's letters to Van Buren and to A. C. Flagg in the respective collections.

[19] For Hawthorne and the *Globe*, see Franklin Pierce to Hawthorne, March 5, 1836, Julian Hawthorne, *Hawthorne and His Wife*, I, 134–135.

[20] See the discussion in Matthiessen, *American Renaissance*, 316–337.

background, it may be illuminating to reopen his case more squarely in terms of the actual issues of the day.[21]

Cooper was basically an upstate New York squire whose politics were determined ultimately by his sense of the security of landed property. His father had been a prominent Federalist; but Cooper early found Jefferson's views on agricultural virtue and popular rule more congenial. By the eighteen-thirties he was ready to believe that Federalist leaders had actually contemplated revolution and monarchy; and in *The Monikins* (1835) he set forth his famous lampoon of Federalism as the "social stake system."[22]

For Cooper, "the heart and strength of the nation" was "its rural population," and the agricultural foundations of the republic seemed to him, as to most Jeffersonians, to be menaced by the commercial community.[23] He was convinced that the "natural antipathy between trade and democracy" was causing businessmen to plot a financial oligarchy. "Most of all," he wrote, "commerce detests popular rights."[24] The history of Britain, fortified by his own experience in France in the early eighteen-thirties, proved the inevitable tendency of business rule toward a moneyed aristocracy. "No government that is essentially influenced by commerce," he concluded, "has ever been otherwise than exclusive, or aristocrat."[25] To his political fears he added the contempt of the landed gentleman for the *parvenu* businessmen. "Of all the sources of human pride," he would write, "mere wealth is the basest and most vulgar minded. Real gentlemen are almost invariably above this low feeling."[26]

These prepossessions, deeply grounded in Cooper's experience, controlled his creative impulses as well as his arguments. The sketches of the Effingham cousins in *Homeward Bound* suggest as vividly as any of his explicit statements Cooper's feelings about the respective effects of owning property in land and in trade. Edward Effingham was "winning in appearance," John "if not positively forbidding, at least distant and repulsive. . . . The noble outline of face in Edward Effingham had got to be cold severity in that of John; the aquiline nose of the latter, seeming to possess an eagle-like and hostile curvature, — his compressed lip, sarcastic and cold expression, . . . a haughty scorn that caused strangers usually to avoid him." What accounted for this differentiation? "Edward Effingham possessed a large hereditary property, that brought a good income, and which attached him to this world of ours by kindly feelings toward its land and water; while John, much the wealthier of the two, having inherited a large commercial fortune, did not own ground enough to bury him. As he sometimes deridingly said, he 'kept his gold in corporations, that were as soulless as himself.' "[27]

[21] Dorothy Waples's valuable *Whig Myth of James Fenimore Cooper* has done much to place Cooper's reputation in proper perspective by showing how he was systematically vilified by the Whig press for his political views. Robert E. Spiller's *Fenimore Cooper: Critic of His Times* develops the general implications of his social criticism. Ethel R. Outland's *The "Effingham" Libels on Cooper* supplies basic information about Cooper's feud with the press. All these books suffer, however, from an imperfect appreciation of the radical extent to which Cooper's views changed from 1834 to 1850.

[22] Cooper, *Sketches of Switzerland* [Part First], II, 158; *Monikins*, 74, 82.

[23] For the quotation, see *Sketches of Switzerland*, Part Second, II, 181.

[24] Cooper, *Gleanings in Europe*, II, 177.

[25] Cooper, *Monikins*, 408; see also *Letter to His Countrymen*, 65–67.

[26] Cooper, *American Democrat*, 131–132; see also *Excursions in Italy*, 184–185.

[27] Cooper, *Homeward Bound*, 12–13.

Cooper's faith in the land and hatred for the financial aristocracy naturally led him, on his return to America in 1833, to become an enthusiastic supporter of the Jackson administration. He adopted the most radical Democratic positions on all questions but the tariff, and was in particular a staunch advocate of the hard-money policy.[28] The rule of property, he said in 1836, is "the most corrupt, narrow and vicious form of polity that has ever been devised."[29] While he had no faith in the infallibility of the whole people, he had even less faith in that of any part of the people. "Though majorities often decide wrong, it is believed that they are less liable to do so than minorities."[30]

In *A Letter to His Countrymen* (1834) he denounced the whole Whig position as an attempt to pervert the American form of government by construing it falsely on British analogies in the hope of ending up with a commercial oligarchy on the British model. *The Monikins* (1835) was a lengthy satirical allegory, at times brilliant, at times tedious, intended to show in more detail in what danger America stood from imitating the business politics of Britain. In both volumes, in the series of travel books he was turning out and in articles for the *New York Evening Post* he attacked the Whig arguments against Jackson's alleged constitutional excesses. In *The American Democrat* (1838) he even defended Jackson's theory of the right of independent adjudication of constitutionality, as developed in the Bank veto.

In his writings throughout the decade, however, there appears beside the approval of Jacksonianism a mounting irritation with the "tyranny of opinion" in America, which, by *The American Democrat* and his novels of 1837 and 1838, *Homeward Bound* and *Home as Found*, was becoming a major theme. Literary historians have interpreted this complaint as evidence of his discomfort under the pressure toward uniformity supposedly exerted by "Jacksonian democracy."

Before accepting this conclusion, it is essential to understand *whose* opinion Cooper was denouncing as tyrannous. In *Sketches of Switzerland* (1836) he declared, "I have never yet been in a country in which what are called the lower orders have not clearer and sounder views than their betters of the great principles which ought to predominate in the control of human affairs." A few pages later, after setting forth a number of routine Democratic arguments in defense of Jackson's use of the presidential power, he commented that current reasoning on these questions "among what are called the enlightened classes" showed how far opinion had lagged behind facts.[31]

There were, in fact, these *two* public opinions for Cooper — that of "what are called the lower orders," which he respected, and that of "what are called the enlightened classes," which he disliked. Yet Cooper was a careless writer, and he could say, immediately after attacks on the "enlightened classes," "I am aware that these are bold opinions to utter in a country where the mass has become so consolidated that it has no longer any integral parts; where the individual is fast losing his individuality in the common identity."[32] In view of the fact that his opinions were "bold" only among "what are called the enlightened classes," it is clear that in this context Cooper's

---

[28] See especially *American Democrat*, 163–165.
[29] *Sketches of Switzerland*, Part Second, I, 36.
[30] *American Democrat*, 46.

[31] *Sketches of Switzerland* [Part First], I, 177, 212.
[32] *Ibid.*, 212.

attack on the "tyranny of opinion" is actually an attack on tyranny of opinion *in his class.*

This is, in fact, the key to his assaults on "tyranny of opinion" in the eighteen-thirties (though not in the eighteen-forties). He would say that if certain progressive opinions were laid before "that portion of the American public which comprises the reading classes," they would have no effect on these classes "on account of their hatred of the rights of the mass"; and in the next sentence he would assert flatly, "I know no country that has retrograded in opinion, so much as our own, within the last five years" — when again he clearly meant, not the whole country, but the "reading classes."[33] "After having passed years in foreign countries, I affirm that I know no state of society in which liberal sentiments are so little relished as in our own, among the upper classes," he would write.[34] But when he began laying about with invective, he tended to forget the qualifications and to accuse the entire nation.

An incident in 1837 intensified Cooper's fears of the "tyranny of opinion." He owned some land on Otsego Lake known as Three Mile Point, which the Coopers had always opened to the village of Cooperstown as a picnic place. In time the villagers began to regard Three Mile Point as public property, and Cooper's attempt to reassert his ownership provoked violent newspaper attacks. Yet it is again hardly just to ascribe these attacks to "Jacksonian democracy." The campaign against Cooper was conducted by the New York Whig press, led by

Thurlow Weed, James Watson Webb, William L. Stone and Horace Greeley, most of whom Cooper later chastised by libel suits, while the Jacksonian press, especially the *New York Evening Post* and the *Albany Argus,* rushed to his defense. "It appears that he is ordained to be hunted down," observed the *New Era,* "The British Whig aristocracy here cry havoc, and their creatures throughout the land echo the cry."[35]

Cooper was, in fact, reacting against a pressure toward uniformity, but it was the pressure, not of mass opinion, but of class opinion. It becomes nonsense to say that Cooper revolted against Jacksonian democracy because of its tyranny over opinion, when actually such tyranny over opinion as he experienced in the eighteen-thirties was provoked in great part by his expression of views favorable to Jacksonian democracy.

Cooper's bitter reaction was reflected in the detailed indictment of public opinion he drew up in *The American Democrat* (1838). But the very points at which he chose to attack public opinion as tyrannous were precisely the points where, as he considered, Whig editors had improperly meddled in his private affairs, and on every current issue discussed he resolutely took the Democratic side. His novels of this period set forth these same emotions. *Home as Found,* though artistically less expert than *Homeward Bound,* was particularly revealing. Like *The American Democrat,* it had two pervading revulsions: on the one hand, the self-constituted aristocracy of the American Whigs, with their pretensions and snobberies, their servility toward the British, their hatred of "that monster" General Jackson and their scorn for the lower classes; on the

---

[33] *Sketches of Switzerland,* Part Second, II, 189–190.

[34] Cooper to Bedford Brown, March 24, 1838, *Historical Papers Published by the Historical Society of Trinity College,* VIII, 2.

[35] *New Era,* June 4, 1840.

ther, the menace of the democratic demagogue.[36]

But the fear of the democratic demagogue did not shake his allegiance to the Democratic party. In New York, in any case, as the Seward-Weed policy gained adherents, the most objectionable demagogues mouthing democratic professions were on the Whig side. "The present political struggle, in this country," he wrote in 1838, "appears to be a contest between men and dollars."[37] The Whig victory of 1840 seemed to him, in his pessimistic later years, "little more than the proof of the power of money and leisure" to make the masses "the instruments of their own subjection."[38] In the campaign of 1844, he attended his first political meeting in twenty-five years, "and if anything could bring me on the stump," he declared vigorously, "it would be to help put down the bold and factious party that is now striving to place Mr. Clay in the chair of state." He denounced the Whig party as "much the falsest and most dangerous association of the sort that has appeared in the country in my day."[39]

Yet Cooper's radicalism was soon to disappear. It was founded, we have seen, in the opposition of landed capital to business capital, the traditional dislike of the *rentier* for the speculator. But in the middle forties Cooper was suddenly asked to decide whether landed property was not in more peril from radicalism than from business. This question was raised sharply by the antirenters, a group of farmers seeking a revision of the semi-

feudal seigneurial relations between patroons and tenants in the huge estates along the Hudson. As a champion of the land, Cooper had rejoiced at the Jacksonian attacks on business; but now demagogues were extending the attack, under the same rallying cries, to the land itself. Would not their victory destroy the foundations of property the nation over? "The existence of true liberty among us, the perpetuity of the institutions, and the safety of public morals, are all dependent on putting down, wholly, absolutely, and unqualifiedly, the false and dishonest theories and statements that have been boldly advanced."[40] From a minor fault of democracy the "demagogue" was becoming a major threat, and the vicious agitators of the antirent trilogy showed Cooper's abhorrence of the class. The trilogy itself, emerging splendidly out of deeply felt and concrete emotions, demonstrated how profoundly Cooper's outlook was rooted in the existing land relationships. His obstinately personal attitude quickly changed any menace to these sacred arrangements into a national calamity.

The antirent troubles did more than shake his belief in popular rule. They destroyed his Jeffersonian faith in the moral infallibility of life on the land. "We do not believe any more," he said, "in the superior innocence and virtue of a rural population."[41] His pessimism deepened. *The Lake Gun* (1850) set forth his fears for the Union, excited inevitably by demagogues; this time he clearly had Seward in mind. Despondency welled up most freely in his last work, *The Towns of Manhattan*. The book itself was destroyed by fire, but the introduction indicates the general temper. If property continued to be assailed,

---

36 For the Jackson reference, *Home as Found*, 123.

37 Cooper to Bedford Brown, March 24, 1838, *loc. cit.*

38 Cooper, *The Redskins*, vi.

39 Cooper to C. A. Secor, *et al.*, September 8, 1844, *The Campaign*, September 21, 1844.

40 Cooper, *Satanstoe*, vii.

41 Cooper, *New York*, 56.

Cooper argued, it would take measures to protect itself. The result might well be fatal to popular liberties, but it would also be the just result of the abuse of popular liberties. There seemed but three possible solutions — military dictatorship, a return to original principles, or "the sway of money."[42] Of the three, the financial aristocracy seemed to him most likely. His old hatred of the commercial oligarchy had weakened, and he recognized it as the only bulwark of property. But his confidence in it was not strong, nor were his hopes for the future bright. This irresolute and baffled conclusion, all the more significant in a man of Cooper's ordinary certainty, suggests the depths of his despair. A year later he was dead.

5

The transcendentalists of Massachusetts constituted the one important literary group never much impressed by Jacksonian democracy. This immunity was all the more singular because for two occasional members, George Bancroft and Orestes A. Brownson, the relations between transcendentalism and democracy seemed close and vital. The Jacksonians, in the minds of Bancroft and Brownson, were carrying on the same revolt against the dead hand of John Locke in politics which the transcendentalists were carrying on in religion. Both Democrat and transcendentalist agreed in asserting the rights of the free mind against the pretensions of precedents or institutions. Both shared a living faith in the integrity and perfectibility of man. Both proclaimed self-reliance. Both detested special groups claiming authority to mediate between the common man and the truth. Both aimed to plant the individual squarely on his instincts, responsible only to himself and

to God. "The soul must and will assert its rightful ascendancy," exclaimed the Bay State Democrat, "over all those arbitrary and conventional forms which a false state of things has riveted upon society." "Democracy," cried Bancroft, "has given to conscience absolute liberty."[43]

But transcendentalism in its Concord form was infinitely individualistic, providing no means for reconciling the diverse intuitions of different men and deciding which was better and which worse. This did not worry most transcendentalists, who would allow Nicholas Biddle the authority of his inner voice and asked only to be allowed equally the authority of their own. The obligations of politics were not so flexible. Bancroft's great modification of transcendentalism was to add that the collective sense of the people provided the indispensable check on the anarchy of individual intuitions. "If reason is a universal faculty, the decision of the common mind is the nearest criterion of truth." Democracy thus perfected the insights of transcendentalism. "Individuals make proclamation of their own fancies; the spirit of God breathes through the combined intelligence of the people. . . . It is, when the multitude give council, that right purposes find safety; theirs is the fixedness that cannot be shaken; theirs is the understanding which exceeds in wisdom."[44]

For Bancroft and Brownson the battle against the past was indivisible, involv-

---

[42] New York, 51.

[43] Bay State Democrat, May 3, 1839; Bancroft, "Address to the Democratic Electors of Massachusetts," Boston Post, October 16, 1835.

[44] Bancroft, "On the Progress of Civilization, or Reasons Why the Natural Association of Men of Letters Is with the Democracy," Boston Quarterly Review, I, 395 (October, 1838); Bancroft, "Address to the Democratic Electors of Massachusetts," Boston Post, October 16, 1835.

ing politics as much as philosophy. In his brilliant chapter on the Quakers in the second volume of his *History* (1837), Bancroft set forth in luminous prose his conception of the relations between the liberation of the soul of man and of his body. For Brownson conservatism in religion and in society were so nearly identical that he could observe of Victor Cousin, the French philosopher, "His works have made many young men among us Democrats." To Cousin himself he proudly declared, "We are combining philosophy with politics," adding that the Democratic party would soon adopt the views of the new school.[45] When Bancroft reviewed George Ripley's *Philosophical Miscellanies,* an anthology of French and German metaphysics, for the *Washington Globe,* he called it "a sort of manifesto of philosophical Democracy," and described how the glory of Jefferson had found new witnesses in the work of Cousin, Jouffroy and Constant.[46] An anonymous essayist in a Democratic paper even admonished the young men, in oddly Emersonian phrases, to "TRUST TO YOURSELF" and hymned the virtues of *"self-dependence."*[47]

Yet, for all the inspiration some Democrats found in transcendentalism, the transcendentalists remained singularly unmoved by the exertions of the Democrats. From their book-lined studies or their shady walks in cool Concord woods, they found the hullabaloo of party politics unedifying and vulgar. The rebuke of Nature was crushing: "So hot? my little Sir." Life was short, and much better to contemplate verities and vibrate

45 Brownson to Bancroft, September 24, 1836, Bancroft Papers; Brownson to Cousin, June 23, 1838, Brownson Papers.

46 *Washington Globe,* March 9, 1838.

47 "To the Young Men," by "H. P.," *Bay State Democrat,* August 16, 1839.

to that iron spring than to make commitments to practicality. A political party, like society itself, was a joint-stock company, in which the members agreed, for the better securing of bread to each shareholder, to surrender the liberty and culture of the eater. "The virtue in most request is conformity. Self-reliance is its aversion."

But for the typical transcendentalist the flinching from politics perhaps expressed a failure they were seeking to erect into a virtue. The exigencies of responsibility were exhausting: much better to demand perfection and indignantly reject the half loaf, than wear out body and spirit in vain grapplings with overmastering reality. The headlong escape into perfection left responsibility far behind for a magic domain where mystic sentiment and gnomic utterance exorcised the rude intrusions of the world. But it was easier to rule the state from Concord than from Washington. And the state had to be ruled, it was the implacable vacuum: if Bronson Alcott preferred Fruitlands, he was not to complain when James K. Polk preferred the White House.

Yet these were the worst, the pure transcendentalists, incapable of effective human relations, terrified of responsibility, given to transforming evasion into a moral triumph. The tougher-minded men on the transcendental margin recognized that certain obligations could not be shaken. The existence of society depended on a mutuality of confidence, the maintenance of which required that the demands of hunger, want and insecurity be met, lest desperation shatter the social chain. These basic agonies were not to be dissolved in the maternal embrace of the oversoul. George Ripley, unlike Bronson Alcott, did not despise those who held the ordinary affairs of life to be important. Whiggery in politics persuaded him as little as Whiggery in religion, and the energy of his friends Bancroft and Brownson stimulated him to work with transcendental insights on the ills of society. "He has fairly philosophized himself into Democracy," wrote Brownson in 1836. Ripley himself bravely declared to Bancroft a year later that "almost to a man, those who shew any marks of genius or intellectual enterprise are philosophical democrats." (The date was September 20, but he had no observations on the independent treasury.) The intellectual ferment of Boston was heady. "There is a great feeding on the mulberry leaves, and it will be hard if silken robes are not woven for the shining ones. . . . I almost hope to see the time, when religion, philosophy and politics will be united in a holy Trinity, for the redemption and blessedness of our social institutions."[48]

But Ripley's gestures toward the Democratic party were those of a pure young man engaged in audacious coquetry with an experienced woman of shady reputation. He smiled, inclined, almost yielded, then snatched away with an air of indignation, his head flushed with the pleasing excitement and his virtue intact. When Bancroft allowed some of Ripley's remarks to fill an anonymous paragraph in the *Boston Post,* Ripley wrote with alarm, "I insist on the distinction between the philosophical principles of democracy, and the democratic party in this country." (His timid advances were being taken with undue seriousness; almost he was invited to meet the family.) ". . . So it is with my young men. They have little faith in par-

ties, but a great zeal for principles. They love nothing about the Whigs but the personal worth which they possess; but they are inclined to doubt whether the opponents of the Whigs are after all true democrats. It is certain, I must confess, that some of the warmest advocates of democratical principles, some who cherish the loftiest faith in the progress of humanity, are found in the Whig ranks."[49] The notes were revealing, for Ripley was not the most innocent of the transcendentalists. Yet he seemed to have no conception at all of, say, the role of measures and policies in underwriting "democratical principles." The diet of mulberry leaves might weave robes for the shining ones, but it gave small nourishment to a realistic view of society.

Ripley had escaped, but his conscience continued peremptory. Then, in 1840, a fairer and more chaste maiden appeared in the vision of Brook Farm, and he was saved from the worldly life of Politics. For him, and for the other transcendentalists who shared his inability to explain away suffering, Brook Farm appeared as a serious solution of the conditions which had driven Bancroft and Brownson into the arms of Party. Their faith was a variant of Utopianism, and Brook Farm appropriately ended up as a Fourierite phalanx.

6

The Oversoul thus comforted the tender transcendentalists, while the tough mowed the hay and raked the dirt at Brook Farm. But beyond the transcendentalists, accepting their inspiration but safe from their illusions, was Emerson, the wisest man of the day. He was too concretely aware of the complexities of

[48] Brownson to Bancroft, September 24, 1836, Ripley to Bancroft, September 20, 1837, Bancroft Papers.

[49] Ripley to Bancroft, November 6, 1837, Bancroft Papers.

experience to be altogether consoled by vagueness and reverie. The doctrine of compensation had its limits, and he was not received by Ripley's community. "At Education Farm, the noblest theory of life sat on the noblest figures of young men and maidens, quite powerless and melancholy. It would not rake or pitch a ton of hay; it would not rub down a horse; and the men and maidens it left pale and hungry."[50] Yet politics represent his greatest failure. He would not succumb to verbal panaceas, neither would he make the ultimate moral effort of Thoreau and cast off all obligation to society. Instead he lingered indecisively, accepting without enthusiasm certain relations to government but never confronting directly the implications of acceptance.

He acknowledged the claims of the Democratic party expounded so ardently by Bancroft and Brownson. "The philosopher, the poet, or the religious man, will, of course, wish to cast his vote with the democrat, for free-trade, for wide suffrage, for the abolition of legal cruelties in the penal code, and for facilitating in every manner the access of the young and the poor to the sources of wealth and power."[51] He recognized, too, the inevitable drift of transcendentalism toward the democratic position. The first lecture of his series in 1839 on the "Present Age" was reported by Theodore Parker as "*Democratic-locofoco* throughout, and very much in the spirit of Brownson's article on Democracy and Reform in the last *Quarterly*." Bancroft left "in ecstasies . . . rapt beyond vision at the *locofocoism*," and one Boston conservative could only growl that Emerson

must be angling for a place in the Custom House.[52]

Yet Emerson would go no farther. "Of the two great parties, which, at this hour, almost share the nation between them," he would lamely conclude, "I should say, that one has the best cause, and the other contains the best men."[53] This would have provided no excuse for inaction, even if it were true, for a man of Emersonian principle should follow his principle; but it was not even true.

Fear of institutions kept him cautious. A party seemed a form of church, and Emerson, a burnt child, shunned the fire. "Bancroft and Bryant," he said, "are historical democrats who are interested in dead or organized, but not in organizing, liberty."[54] He liked the *Washington Globe's* motto — "The world is governed too much" — though it appalled him that so many people read the paper. But in an imperfect world, should he not settle for "historical democrats" and *Washington Globes*, or at least remark on the alternative? Emerson was well aware of the discipline of choice. Yet here he failed himself, and ignored the responsibilities of his own moral position.

Fundamentally he did not care, and thus he was betrayed, almost without struggle, into the clichés of conservatism which had surrounded him from birth. In a flash of insight he could see that "banks and tariffs, the newspaper and caucus" were "flat and dull to dull people, but rest on the same foundations of wonder as the town of Troy, and the temple of Delphos."[55] Yet, in life at Con-

---

[50] Emerson, *Essays* (World's Classics), 300.

[51] *Essays*, 407–408.

[52] Parker to Convers Francis, December 6, 1839, J. E. Cabot, *Memoir of Ralph Waldo Emerson*, 400–401.

[53] *Essays*, 407.

[54] *Journals*, VI, 315.

[55] *Essays*, 285.

cord, day in, day out, banks and tariffs were flat and dull to him. As he glanced at party contests, he was most impressed by "the meanness of our politics."[56]

He had little idea of the significance of the struggles of the eighteen-thirties. His ejaculation to Carlyle in 1834 — "a most unfit man in the Presidency has been doing the worst things" — about exhausted his conception of the Jackson administration.[57] His reluctance to break with the Whigs was increased by his invention of a statesman named Daniel Webster to whom he gave profound devotion and whom he carelessly confused with the popular Whig politician of the same name. "That great forehead which I followed about all my young days, from court-house to senate chamber, from caucus to street" cast a hypnotic spell over a man otherwise hard to fool.[58] His comments, scattered over two decades of loyalty, show a literary fascination with the massiveness of personality, the stately rhetoric, the marble brow and face black as thunder; but little concern for his views on practical policy. This Webster was a mirage peculiar to Emerson. For Bryant, Bancroft, Cooper, Whitman and Hawthorne, Webster was the most vulnerable celebrity of the day.[59] But for Emerson he remained a great statesman — until Webster finally ran up against an issue which really excited

Emerson's imagination and commanded his full attention, and the speech on the Compromise of 1850 disclosed to Emerson what he should have known for years. The steady wisdom of the sage of Concord faltered, in this one field, into sentimentality.

7

Of all the New England group who shunned political choice, Thoreau alone lived at a degree of moral tension which imposed responsibilities equivalent to those borne by men who sought to govern. He could not delude himself with fantasies of easy salvation, like Alcott or Ripley, nor could he accept the status of citizenship, like Emerson, and dally with its obligations. For him the moral life admitted but one possibility: the complete assumption of all responsibility by the individual. The highest good, said Thoreau, was the living unity of the ethical consciousness and its direct, solid expression in art and life.

In practice he achieved the goal best by a deliberate reduction of life to its essentials — a cabin by blue Walden, blackberries in the summer, the indomitable woodchuck, the wild sweet song of the evening robin, the geese flying low over the woods, the last blaze of sun in the west. But he could not dwell forever at Walden; he had other lives to live; and he returned to society, now fulfilling

---

[56] *Essays*, 185.

[57] Emerson to Carlyle, May 14, 1834, *Correspondence of Thomas Carlyle and Ralph Waldo Emerson, 1843–1872*, C. E. Norton, ed., I, 16.

[58] Emerson to Carlyle, August 8, 1839, *ibid.*, I, 255.

[59] Webster was the butt of the Democratic literary men, as his peculiar combination of cynicism and external moral grandeur made inevitable. Hawthorne's sketch of Webster as "Old Stony Phiz" in "The Great Stone Face" is well-known and penetrating, presenting him as "a man of mighty faculties and little aims, whose life, with

all its high performances, was vague and empty, because no high purpose had endowed it with reality." Hawthorne, *Writings*, III, 51. For Bancroft's ribald running comment on Webster, see his correspondence with Van Buren. Bryant's famous editorial on Webster's humor in the *New York Evening Post* of November 20, 1837, is to be found in Bryant, *Prose Writings*, Parke Godwin, ed., II, 383–385. A typical Cooper reference is in *The Monikins*, 414. Whitman summed them all up with his brief remark that Webster was "overrated more than any other public man ever prominent in America." *Brooklyn Eagle*, April 11, 1846, *Gathering of the Forces*, II, 182.

his singleness of feeling by fusing his superb style till the words, as he said, fell like boulders across the page. Back in the world again, he was face to face with the enemies of the moral life: the new industrialism, which would deform the moral self, and the state, which would corrupt it. In society people lived in quiet desperation, sick at heart, their integrity menaced, clouded and compromised. The only man worth having, thought Thoreau, was the man of principle, and he was worth any expense to the state.

The state, he said, had no moral status. Its rule was expediency, its method, force. It had no right to act on its subjects in terms of obligation and duty. Individuals could have no moral relation to it: the soul was indefeasible, and its burdens could not be assumed by the state. Men should tolerate the state in its milder moments, but, when it seeks to violate their integrity by immoral actions of its own, they must shake themselves free of all complicity. "The only government that I recognize — and it matters not how few are at the head of it, or how small its army — is that power that establishes justice in the land, never that which establishes injustice." Was not the presumption always against the state, that "semihuman tiger or ox, stalking over the earth, with its heart taken out and the top of its brain shot away"? "Is it not possible," he cried, "that an individual may be right and a government wrong?" Man must achieve his moral unity, if necessary at the cost of civil disobedience. This was the sublimest heroism; "for once we are lifted out of the trivialness and dust of politics into the region of truth and manhood." Only a succession of *men*, carrying out such defiances, could tame the semihuman

tiger till the state should recognize the individual "as a higher and independent power, from which all its own power and authority are derived, and treats him accordingly."[60]

Thoreau's case was consistent and irrevocable. It was his by bitter conquest, and into holding it he poured the energies of his life. No position could be more exhausting and more pitiless. The relentless pressure of everlasting responsibility beat down on the frail individual, deprived of the possibility of diffusing his guilt among society, alone against the universe, armed only with his own inner righteousness.

Few men could stand the unimaginable strain: for most it leads to hypocrisy or collapse. "Man is neither angel nor brute," observed Pascal, "and the unfortunate thing is that he who would act the angel acts the brute." It is for this reason that society has proscribed those evaders who claim the prerogatives of a Thoreau without undergoing his intense moral ordeal. Civil disobedience is justified only by the sternest private obedience, and angels are all too likely to turn into brutes. Thoreau earned his beliefs and his immunities. Little men, covering cowardice with a veil of self-righteousness, lay claim to the exemptions of a Thoreau with the most intolerable pretense. The camp followers of a war which he fought, they are presently the camp followers of a war fought by the rest of society, accepting the protection of the state but disclaiming any obligations. Their performance should not compromise his case. The writings and life of Thoreau presented democracy with a profound moral challenge.

[60] Thoreau, "Plea for Captain John Brown," *Works*, IV, 430, 429, 437; "Civil Disobedience," *Works*, IV, 387.

8

Thoreau said Nay to the claims of democracy, but Walt Whitman sent back the thunderous affirmation, echoing off the roof-tops of the world. Twenty-one in the year of Tippecanoe, Whitman was already up to his neck in radical Democratic politics. In a year, he would be speaking at a huge party mass meeting and contributing to the *Democratic Review*. In 1844 he would join the movement to draft Silas Wright for Governor and elect James K. Polk. In 1846 he would become editor of the *Brooklyn Daily Eagle,* and while in Brooklyn serve on the Democratic General Committee and the Fourth of July Celebration Committee.

Brooklyn knew him as Walter Whitman, an amiable and relaxed young man, with a ruddy pleasant face and a short beard, wandering indolently through the bustling streets with an easy word for everyone, from merchant to cartman. After his stint for the *Eagle* he would go down to Gray's Swimming Bath at the foot of Fulton Street and lounge for twenty minutes in the water. Then the office boy would give him a shower, and he would take the evening ferry back to New York through the dying sunset.[61] ("Flood-tide below me! I see you face to face! Clouds of the west — sun there half an hour high — I see you also face to face.")

These were days of quiet immersion in the flood of experience which would later sweep aside the conventions of verse to achieve their own expression, poignant, tender, gusty, barbaric, incoherent and magnificent. He drank in not just the sea gulls, floating high in the air on motionless wings, their bodies lit up

[61] Whitman, *Gathering of the Forces,* I, xix–xxiii.

glistening yellow by the setting sun, not just the men and women on the street, "the blab of the pave, tires of carts, sluff of boot-soles, talk of the promenaders." He drank in the feelings of the people themselves, their anxieties, hopes, aspirations.

For Whitman none of the doubts of Thoreau. For him only a vigorous acceptance and mastery of the democratic opportunity. "To attack the turbulence and destructiveness of the Democratic spirit," he said, "is an old story. . . . Why, all that is good and grand in any political organization in the world, is the result of this turbulence and destructiveness; and controlled by the intelligence and common sense of such a people as the Americans, it never has brought harm, and never can."

Politics a noisy show, unworthy of the attention of serious men? "It is the fashion of a certain set to assume to despise 'politics' . . . they look at the fierce struggle, and at the battle of principles and candidates, and their weak nerves retreat dismayed from the neighborhood of such scenes of convulsion. But to our view, the spectacle is always a grand one — full of the most august and sublime attributes."

The enthusiasm of democracy an evil? "All the noisy tempestuous scenes of politics witnessed in this country — all the excitement and strife, even — are *good* to behold. They evince that the *people act;* they are the discipline of the young giant, getting his maturer strength."

Is democracy then perfect? Let no one be distracted by detail. "We know, well enough, that the workings of Democracy are not always justifiable, in every trivial point. But the great winds that purify the air, without which nature would flag into ruin — are they to be condemned because a tree is prostrated here and there, in their course?"[62]

Through the blast of Whitman's prose sounded the answer to Thoreau. Man, he affirmed, could have a relation of moral significance to the state, so long as the state was truly the expression of the popular will and the best in man. Perfection? No, for the state, like the people which created it, had failings and flaws. (Whitman, unlike Thoreau, had a certain sympathy for imperfections.) Belief in the people should not be discouraged by trivialities or weakened by petty disappointments. In the greatness of his faith in the people Whitman could not but declare his faith in the possibilities of democratic government.

In 1856 Henry Thoreau and Walt Whitman, meeting for the first time, had a stiff conversation in Whitman's attic study in New York. Thoreau felt that he did not get very far. "Among the few things which I chanced to say, I remember that one was . . . that I did not think much of America or of politics, and so on, which may have been somewhat of a damper to him." No doubt it was, and Whitman carried away a vivid impression of Thoreau's "disdain for men (for Tom, Dick, and Harry): inability to appreciate the average life — even the exceptional life: it seemed to me a want of imagination. He couldn't put his life into any other life — realize why one man was so and another was not so: was impatient with other people on the street and so forth." They had, as Whitman

recalled it, rather a hot discussion. "It was a bitter difference: it was rather a surprise to me to meet in Thoreau such a very aggravated case of superciliousness."[63]

Thoreau himself contemplated no social reconstruction. He simply wanted to live his own life under standards higher than men like Whitman, who could put off some of their own guilt on the rest of society. But the mass of men must live in society, or in their visions of a new society; and while there is room for superciliousness in a democracy, it provides an inadequate basis for a political philosophy. The impulse of Whitman was healthier for the social state. His life was spent in an exultation in the potentialities, and a scourging of the failures, of democracy. If the state was not to be a semihuman tiger, with its heart taken out and the top of its brain shot away, it would probably be due more to the Whitmans than to the Thoreaus. As Whitman himself declared, "There is no week nor day nor hour when tyranny may not enter upon this country, if the people lose their supreme confidence in themselves, — and lose their roughness and spirit of defiance — Tyranny may always enter — there is no charm no bar against it — the only bar against it is a large resolute breed of men."[64]

[62] Whitman, "American Democracy," *Brooklyn Eagle*, April 20, 1847, *Gathering of the Forces*, I, 3–6.

[63] Thoreau to Harrison Blake, December 7, 1856, *Works*, XI, 347; Traubel, *With Whitman in Camden*, I, 212. See also H. S. Canby, *Thoreau*, 412–417.

[64] "Notes for Lectures on Democracy and 'Adhesiveness,' " C. J. Furness, *Walt Whitman's Workshop*, 58.

Ralph Waldo Emerson:
THE TRANSCENDENTALIST

THE first thing we have to say respecting what are called *new views* here in New England, at the present time, is, that they are not new, but the very oldest of thoughts cast into the mould of these new times. The light is always identical in its composition, but it falls on a great variety of objects, and by so falling is first revealed to us, not in its own form, for it is formless, but in theirs; in like manner, thought only appears in the objects it classifies. What is popularly called Transcendentalism among us, is Idealism; Idealism as it appears in 1842. As thinkers, mankind have ever divided into two sects, Materialists and Idealists; the first class founding on experience, the second on consciousness; the first class beginning to think from the data of the senses, the second class perceive that the senses are not final, and say, The senses give us representations of things, but what are the things themselves, they cannot tell. The materialist insists on facts, on history, on the force of circumstances and the animal wants of man; the idealist on the power of Thought and of Will, on inspiration, on miracle, on individual culture. These two modes of thinking are both natural, but the idealist contends that his way of thinking is in higher nature. He concedes all that the other affirms, admits the impressions of sense, admits their coherency, their use and beauty, and then asks the materialist for his grounds of assurance that things are as his senses represent them. But I, he says, affirm facts not affected by the illusions of sense, facts which are of the same nature as the faculty which reports them, and not liable to doubt; facts which in their first appearance to us assume a native superiority to material facts, degrading these into a language by which the first are to be spoken; facts which it only needs a retirement from the senses to discern. Every materialist will be an idealist; but an idealist can never go backward to be a materialist.

The idealist, in speaking of events, sees them as spirits. He does not deny the sensuous fact: by no means; but he will not see that alone. He does not deny the presence of this table, this chair, and the walls of this room, but he looks at these things as the reverse side of the tapestry, as the *other end,* each being a sequel or completion of a spiritual fact which nearly concerns him. This manner of looking at things transfers every object in nature from an independent and anomalous position without there, into the consciousness. Even the materialist Condillac, perhaps the most logical expounder of materialism, was constrained to say, "Though we should soar into the heavens, though we should sink into the abyss, we never go out of ourselves; it is always our own thought that we perceive." What more could an idealist say?

The materialist, secure in the certainty
f sensation, mocks at fine-spun theories,
t star-gazers and dreamers, and believes
hat his life is solid, that he at least takes
.othing for granted, but knows where he
tands, and what he does. Yet how easy
t is to show him that he also is a phan-
om walking and working amid phan-
oms, and that he need only ask a ques-
ion or two beyond his daily questions
o find his solid universe growing dim
nd impalpable before his sense. The
turdy capitalist, no matter how deep
nd square on blocks of Quincy granite
e lays the foundations of his banking-
.ouse or Exchange, must set it, at last,
ot on a cube corresponding to the
ngles of his structure, but on a mass of
nknown materials and solidity, red-hot
r white-hot perhaps at the core, which
ounds off to an almost perfect spheric-
ty, and lies floating in soft air, and
oes spinning away, dragging bank and
anker with it at a rate of thousands of
iles the hour, he knows not whither, —
bit of bullet, now glimmering, now
arkling through a small cubic space on
he edge of an unimaginable pit of empti-
ess. And this wild balloon, in which
is whole venture is embarked, is a just
ymbol of his whole state and faculty.
ne thing at least, he says, is certain,
nd does not give me the headache, that
gures do not lie; the multiplication table
as been hitherto found unimpeachable
ruth; and, moreover, if I put a gold
agle in my safe, I find it again to-
norrow; — but for these thoughts, I know
ot whence they are. They change and
ass away. But ask him why he believes
hat an uniform experience will continue
niform, or on what grounds he founds
is faith in his figures, and he will per-
eive that his mental fabric is built up
n just as strange and quaking founda-
ions as his proud edifice of stone.

In the order of thought, the materialist
takes his departure from the external
world, and esteems a man as one product
of that. The idealist takes his departure
from his consciousness, and reckons the
world an appearance. The materialist
respects sensible masses, Society, Government, social art and luxury, every
establishment, every mass, whether majority of numbers, or extent of space, or
amount of objects, every social action.
The idealist has another measure, which
is metaphysical, namely the *rank* which
things themselves take in his consciousness; not at all the size or appearance.
Mind is the only reality, of which men
and all other natures are better or worse
reflectors. Nature, literature, history, are
only subjective phenomena. Although in
his action overpowered by the laws of
action, and so, warmly cooperating with
men, even preferring them to himself,
yet when he speaks scientifically, or after
the order of thought, he is constrained
to degrade persons into representatives
of truths. He does not respect labor, or
the products of labor, namely property,
otherwise than as a manifold symbol,
illustrating with wonderful fidelity of
details the laws of being; he does not
respect government, except as far as it
reiterates the law of his mind; nor the
church, nor charities, nor arts, for themselves; but hears, as at a vast distance,
what they say, as if his consciousness
would speak to him through a panto-
mimic scene. His thought, — that is the
Universe. His experience inclines him
to behold the procession of facts you
call the world, as flowing perpetually
outward from an invisible, unsounded
centre in himself, centre alike of him and
of them, and necessitating him to regard
all things as having a subjective or relative existence, relative to that aforesaid
Unknown Centre of him.

From this transfer of the world into the consciousness, this beholding of all things in the mind, follow easily his whole ethics. It is simpler to be self-dependent. The height, the deity of man is to be self-sustained, to need no gift, no foreign force. Society is good when it does not violate me, but best when it is likest to solitude. Everything real is self-existent. Everything divine shares the self-existence of Deity. All that you call the world is the shadow of that substance which you are, the perpetual creation of the powers of thought, of those that are dependent and of those that are independent of your will. Do not cumber yourself with fruitless pains to mend and remedy remote effects; let the soul be erect, and all things will go well. You think me the child of my circumstances: I make my circumstance. Let any thought or motive of mine be different from that they are, the difference will transform my condition and economy. I — this thought which is called I — is the mould into which the world is poured like melted wax. The mould is invisible, but the world betrays the shape of the mould. You call it the power of circumstance, but it is the power of me. Am I in harmony with myself? my position will seem to you just and commanding. Am I vicious and insane? my fortunes will seem to you obscure and descending. As I am, so shall I associate, and so shall I act; Caesar's history will paint out Caesar. Jesus acted so, because he thought so. I do not wish to overlook or to gainsay any reality; I say I make my circumstance; but if you ask me, Whence am I? I feel like other men my relation to that Fact which cannot be spoken, or defined, nor even thought, but which exists, and will exist.

The Transcendentalist adopts the whole connection of spiritual doctrine.

He believes in miracle, in the perpetual openness of the human mind to new influx of light and power; he believes in inspiration, and in ecstasy. He wishes that the spiritual principle should be suffered to demonstrate itself to the end in all possible applications to the state of man, without the admission of anything unspiritual; that is, anything positive, dogmatic, personal. Thus the spiritual measure of inspiration is the depth of the thought, and never, who said it. And so he resists all attempts to palm other rules and measures on the spirit than its own.

In action he easily incurs the charge of antinomianism by his avowal that he who has the Lawgiver, may with safety not only neglect, but even contravene every written commandment. In the play of Othello, the expiring Desdemona absolves her husband of the murder, to her attendant Emilia. Afterwards, when Emilia charges him with the crime, Othello exclaims, "You heard her say herself it was not I." Emilia replies, "The more angel she, and thou the blacker devil."

Of this fine incident, Jacobi, the Transcendental moralist, makes use, with other parallel instances, in his reply to Fichte. Jacobi, refusing all measure of right and wrong except the determinations of the private spirit, remarks that there is no crime but has sometimes been a virtue. "I," he says, "am that atheist, that godless person who, in opposition to an imaginary doctrine of calculation, would lie as the dying Desdemona lied; would lie and deceive, as Pylades when he personated Orestes; would assassinate like Timoleon; would perjure myself like Epaminondas and John de Witt; I would resolve on suicide like Cato; I would commit sacrilege with David; yea, and pluck ears of corn on the Sabbath, for o other reason than that I was fainting or lack of food. For I have assurance in myself that in pardoning these faults according to the letter, man exerts the sovereign right which the majesty of his being confers on him; he sets the seal of his divine nature to the grace he accords."

In like manner, if there is anything grand and daring in human thought or virtue, any reliance on the vast, the unknown; any presentiment, any extravagance of faith, the spiritualist adopts it as most in nature. The oriental mind has always tended to this largeness. Buddhism is an expression of it. The Buddhist, who thanks no man, who says 'Do not flatter your benefactors," but who, in his conviction that every good deed can by no possibility escape its reward, will not deceive the benefactor by pretending that he has done more than he should, is a Transcendentalist.

You will see by this sketch that there is no such thing as a Transcendental *party;* that there is no pure Transcendentalist; that we know of none but prophets and heralds of such a philosophy; that all who by strong bias of nature have leaned to the spiritual side in doctrine, have stopped short of their goal. We have had many harbingers and forerunners; but of a purely spiritual life, history has afforded no example. I mean we have yet no man who has leaned entirely on his character, and eaten angels' food; who, trusting to his sentiments, found life made of miracles; who, working for universal aims, found himself fed, he knew not how; clothed, sheltered, and weaponed, he knew not how, and yet it was done by his own hands. Only in the instinct of the lower animals we find the suggestion of the methods of it, and something higher than our understanding. The squirrel hoards nuts and the bee gathers honey, without knowing what they do, and they are thus provided for without selfishness or disgrace.

Shall we say then that Transcendentalism is the Saturnalia or excess of Faith; the presentiment of a faith proper to man in his integrity, excessive only when his imperfect obedience hinders the satisfaction of his wish? Nature is transcendental, exists primarily, necessarily, ever works and advances, yet takes no thought for the morrow. Man owns the dignity of the life which throbs around him, in chemistry, and tree, and animal, and in the involuntary functions of his own body; yet he is balked when he tries to fling himself into this enchanted circle, where all is done without degradation. Yet genius and virtue predict in man the same absence of private ends and of condescension to circumstances, united with every trait and talent of beauty and power.

This way of thinking, falling on Roman times, made Stoic philosophers; falling on despotic times, made patriot Catos and Brutuses; falling on superstitious times, made prophets and apostles; on popish times, made protestants and ascetic monks, preachers of Faith against the preachers of Works; on prelatical times, made Puritans and Quakers; and falling on Unitarian and commercial times, makes the peculiar shades of Idealism which we know.

It is well known to most of my audience that the Idealism of the present day acquired the name of Transcendental from the use of that term by Immanuel Kant, of Königsberg, who replied to the skeptical philosophy of Locke, which insisted that there was nothing in the intellect which was not previously in the experience of the senses, by showing that there was a very important class of ideas or imperative forms, which did not come by experience, but through which experience was acquired; that these were intuitions of the mind itself; and he denominated them *Transcendental* forms. The extraordinary profoundness and precision of that man's thinking have given vogue to his nomenclature, in Europe and America, to that extent that whatever belongs to the class of intuitive thought is popularly called at the present day *Transcendental*.

Although, as we have said, there is no pure Transcendentalist, yet the tendency to respect the intuitions and to give them, at least in our creed, all authority over our experience, has deeply colored the conversation and poetry of the present day; and the history of genius and of religion in these times, though impure, and as yet not incarnated in any powerful individual, will be the history of this tendency.

It is a sign of our times, conspicuous to the coarsest observer, that many intelligent and religious persons withdraw themselves from the common labors and competitions of the market and the caucus, and betake themselves to a certain solitary and critical way of living, from which no solid fruit has yet appeared to justify their separation. They hold themselves aloof: they feel the disproportion between their faculties and the work offered them, and they prefer to ramble in the country and perish of ennui, to the degradation of such charities and such ambitions as the city can propose to them. They are striking work, and crying out for somewhat worthy to do! What they do is done only because they are overpowered by the humanities that speak on all sides; and they consent to such labor as is open to them, though to their lofty dream the writing of Iliads

or Hamlets, or the building of cities c empires seems drudgery.

Now every one must do after his kin be he asp or angel, and these must. Th question which a wise man and a studer of modern history will ask, is, what tha kind is? And truly, as in ecclesiastic; history we take so much pains to knov what the Gnostics, what the Essene: what the Manichees, and what the Re formers believed, it would not misbe come us to inquire nearer home, wha these companions and contemporaries o ours think and do, at least so far as thes: thoughts and actions appear to be no accidental and personal, but common t: many, and the inevitable flower of th: Tree of Time. Our American literature and spiritual history are, we confess, i: the optative mood; but whoso know these seething brains, these admirable radicals, these unsocial worshippers these talkers who talk the sun and moor away, will believe that this heresy can not pass away without leaving its mark.

They are lonely; the spirit of their writing and conversation is lonely; they repel influences; they shun general society; they incline to shut themselves in their chamber in the house, to live in the country rather than in the town, and to find their tasks and amusements in solitude. Society, to be sure, does not like this very well; it saith, Whoso goes to walk alone, accuses the whole world; he declares all to be unfit to be his companions; it is very uncivil, nay, insulting; Society will retaliate. Meantime, this retirement does not proceed from any whim on the part of these separators; but if any one will take pains to talk with them, he will find that this part is chosen both from temperament and from principle; with some unwillingness too, and as a choice of the less of two evils;

for these persons are not by nature melancholy, sour, and unsocial, — they are not stockish or brute, — but joyous, susceptible, affectionate; they have even more than others a great wish to be loved. Like the young Mozart, they are rather ready to cry ten times a day, "But are you sure you love me?" Nay, if they tell you their whole thought, they will own that love seems to them the last and highest gift of nature; that there are persons whom in their hearts they daily thank for existing, — persons whose faces are perhaps unknown to them, but whose fame and spirit have penetrated their solitude, — and for whose sake they wish to exist. To behold the beauty of another character, which inspires a new interest in our own; to behold the beauty lodged in a human being, with such vivacity of apprehension that I am instantly forced home to inquire if I am not deformity itself; to behold in another the expression of a love so high that it assures itself, — assures itself also to me against every possible casualty except my unworthiness; — these are degrees on the scale of human happiness to which they have ascended; and it is a fidelity to this sentiment which has made common association distasteful to them. They wish a just and even fellowship, or none. They cannot gossip with you, and they do not wish, as they are sincere and religious, to gratify any mere curiosity which you may entertain. Like fairies, they do not wish to be spoken of. Love me, they say, but do not ask who is my cousin and my uncle. If you do not need to hear my thought, because you can read it in my face and behavior, then I will tell it you from sunrise to sunset. If you cannot divine it, you would not understand what I say. I will not molest myself for you. I do not wish to be profaned.

And yet, it seems as if this loneliness, and not this love, would prevail in their circumstances, because of the extravagant demand they make on human nature. That, indeed, constitutes a new feature in their portrait, that they are the most exacting and extortionate critics. Their quarrel with every man they meet is not with his kind, but with his degree. There is not enough of him, — that is the only fault. They prolong their privilege of childhood in this wise; of doing nothing, but making immense demands on all the gladiators in the lists of action and fame. They make us feel the strange disappointment which overcasts every human youth. So many promising youths, and never a finished man! The profound nature will have a savage rudeness; the delicate one will be shallow, or the victim of sensibility; the richly accomplished will have some capital absurdity; and so every piece has a crack. 'Tis strange, but this masterpiece is the result of such an extreme delicacy that the most unobserved flaw in the boy will neutralize the most aspiring genius, and spoil the work. Talk with a seaman of the hazards to life in his profession and he will ask you, "Where are the old sailors? Do you not see that all are young men?" And we, on this sea of human thought, in like manner inquire, Where are the old idealists? where are they who represented to the last generation that extravagant hope which a few happy aspirants suggest to ours? In looking at the class of counsel, and power, and wealth, and at the matronage of the land, amidst all the prudence and all the triviality, one asks, Where are they who represented genius, virtue, the invisible and heavenly world, to these? Are they dead, — taken in early ripeness to the gods, — as ancient wisdom foretold their fate? Or did the high idea die out of them, and leave their unperfumed body as its tomb and tablet, announcing to all that the celestial inhabitant, who once gave them beauty, had departed? Will it be better with the new generation? We easily predict a fair future to each new candidate who enters the lists, but we are frivolous and volatile, and by low aims and ill example do what we can to defeat this hope. Then these youths bring us a rough but effectual aid. By their unconcealed dissatisfaction they expose our poverty and the insignificance of man to man. A man is a poor limitary benefactor. He ought to be a shower of benefits — a great influence, which should never let his brother go, but should refresh old merits continually with new ones; so that though absent he should never be out of my mind, his name never far from my lips; but if the earth should open at my side, or my last hour were come, his name should be the prayer I should utter to the Universe. But in our experience, man is cheap and friendship wants its deep sense. We affect to dwell with our friends in their absence, but we do not; when deed, word, or letter comes not, they let us go. These exacting children advertise us of our wants. There is no compliment, no smooth speech with them; they pay you only this one compliment, of insatiable expectation; they aspire, they severely exact, and if they only stand fast in this watch-tower, and persist in demanding unto the end, and without end, then are they terrible friends, whereof poet and priest cannot choose but stand in awe; and what if they eat clouds, and drink wind, they have not been without service to the race of man.

With this passion for what is great and extraordinary, it cannot be wondered at that they are repelled by vulgarity and frivolity in people. They say to themselves, It is better to be alone than in bad company. And it is really a wish to be met, — the wish to find society for their hope and religion, — which prompts them to shun what is called society. They feel that they are never so fit for friendship as when they have quitted mankind and taken themselves to friend. A picture, a book, a favorite spot in the hills or the woods which they can people with the fair and worthy creation of the fancy, can give them often forms so vivid that these for the time shall seem real, and society the illusion.

But their solitary and fastidious manners not only withdraw them from the conversation, but from the labors of the world; they are not good citizens, not good members of society; unwillingly they bear their part of the public and private burdens; they do not willingly share in the public charities, in the public religious rites, in the enterprises of education, of missions foreign and domestic, in the abolition of the slave-trade, or in the temperance society. They do not even like to vote. The philanthropists inquire whether Transcendentalism does not mean sloth: they had as lief hear that their friend is dead, as that he is a Transcendentalist; for then is he paralyzed, and can never do anything for humanity. What right, cries the good world, has the man of genius to retreat from work, and indulge himself? The popular literary creed seems to be, "I am a sublime genius; I ought not therefore to labor." But genius is the power to labor better and more availably. Deserve thy genius: exalt it. The good, the illuminated, sit apart from the rest, censuring their dulness and vices, as if they thought that by sitting very grand in their chairs, the very brokers, attorneys, and congressmen would see the error of their ways, and flock to them. But the good and wise must learn to act, and carry salvation to the combatants and demagogues in the dusty arena below.

On the part of these children it is replied that life and their faculty seem to them gifts too rich to be squandered on such trifles as you propose to them. What you call your fundamental institutions, your great and holy causes, seem to them great abuses, and, when nearly seen, paltry matters. Each "cause" as it is called, — say Abolition, Temperance, say Calvinism, or Unitarianism, — becomes speedily a little shop, where the article, let it have been at first never so subtle and ethereal, is now made up into portable and convenient cakes, and retailed in small quantities to suit purchasers. You make very free use of these words "great" and "holy," but few things appear to them such. Few persons have any magnificence of nature to inspire enthusiasm, and the philanthropies and charities have a certain air of quackery. As to the general course of living, and the daily employments of men, they cannot see much virtue in these, since they are parts of this vicious circle; and as no great ends are answered by the men, there is nothing noble in the arts by which they are maintained. Nay, they have made the experiment and found that from the liberal professions to the coarsest manual labor, and from the courtesies of the academy and the college to the conventions of the cotillon-room and the morning call, there is a spirit of cowardly compromise and seeming which intimates a frightful skepticism, a life without love, and an activity without an aim.

Unless the action is necessary, unless it is adequate, I do not wish to perform it. I do not wish to do one thing but once. I do not love routine. Once possessed of the principle, it is equally easy to make four or forty thousand applications of it. A great man will be content to have indicated in any the slightest manner his perception of the reigning Idea of his time, and will leave to those who like it the multiplication of examples. When he has hit the white, the rest may shatter the target. Every thing admonishes us how needlessly long life is. Every moment of a hero so raises and cheers us that a twelve-month is an age. All that the brave Xanthus brings home from his wars is the recollection that at the storming of Samos, "in the heat of the battle, Pericles smiled on me, and passed on to another detachment." It is the quality of the moment, not the number of days, of events, or of actors, that imports.

New, we confess, and by no means happy, is our condition: if you want the aid of our labor, we ourselves stand in greater want of the labor. We are miserable with inaction. We perish of rest and rust: but we do not like your work.

"Then," says the world, "show me your own."

"We have none."

"What will you do, then?" cries the world.

"We will wait."

"How long?"

"Until the Universe beckons and calls us to work."

"But whilst you wait, you grow old and useless."

"Be it so: I can sit in a corner and *perish* (as you call it), but I will not move until I have the highest command. If no call should come for years, for centuries, then I know that the want of the Universe is the attestation of faith by my abstinence. Your virtuous projects, so called, do not cheer me. I know that which shall come will cheer me. If I cannot work at least I need not lie. All that is clearly due to-day is not to lie. In other places other men have encountered sharp trials, and have behaved themselves well. The martyrs were sawn asunder, or hung alive on meathooks. Cannot we screw our courage to patience and truth, and without complaints, or even with good-humor, await our turn of action in the Infinite Counsels?"

But to come a little closer to the secret of these persons, we must say that to them it seems a very easy matter to answer the objections of the man of the world, but not so easy to dispose of the doubts and objections that occur to themselves. They are exercised in their own spirit with queries which acquaint them with all adversity, and with the trials of the bravest heroes. When I asked them concerning their private experience, they answered somewhat in this wise: It is not to be denied that there must be some wide difference between my faith and other faith; and mine is a certain brief experience, which surprised me in the highway or in the market, in some place, at some time, — whether in the body or out of the body, God knoweth, — and made me aware that I had played the fool with fools all this time, but that law existed for me and for all; that to me belonged trust, a child's trust and obedience, and the worship of ideas, and I should never be fool more. Well, in the space of an hour probably, I was let down from this height; I was at my old tricks, the selfish member of a selfish society. My life is superficial, takes no root in the deep world; I ask, When shall I die and be relieved of the responsibility of seeing an Universe which I do not use? I wish to exchange this flash-of-lightning faith for continuous daylight, this fever-glow for a benign climate.

These two states of thought diverge every moment, and stand in wild contrast. To him who looks at his life from these moments of illumination, it will seem that he skulks and plays a mean, shiftless and subaltern part in the world. That is to be done which he has not skill to do, or to be said which others can say better, and he lies by, or occupies his hands with some plaything, until his hour comes again. Much of our reading, much of our labor, seems mere waiting: it was not that we were born for. Any other could do it as well or better. So little skill enters into these works, so little do they mix with the divine life, that it really signifies little what we do, whether we turn a grindstone, or ride, or run, or make fortunes, or govern the state. The worst feature of this double consciousness is, that the two lives, of the understanding and of the soul, which we lead, really show very little relation to each other; never meet and measure each other: one prevails now, all buzz and din; and the other prevails then, all infinitude and paradise; and, with the progress of life, the two discover no greater disposition to reconcile themselves. Yet, what is my faith? What am I? What but a thought of serenity and independence, an abode in the deep blue sky? Presently the clouds shut down again; yet we retain the belief that this petty web we weave will at last be overshot and reticulated with veins of the blue, and that the moments will characterize the days. Patience, then, is for us, is it not? Patience, and still patience. When we pass, as presently we shall, into some new infinitude, out of this Iceland of negations, it will please us to reflect that though we had few virtues or consolations, we bore with our indigence, nor once strove to repair it with hypocrisy or false heat of any kind.

But this class are not sufficiently characterized if we omit to add that they are lovers and worshippers of Beauty. In the eternal trinity of Truth, Goodness, and Beauty, each in its perfection including the three, they prefer to make Beauty the sign and head. Something of the same taste is observable in all the moral movements of the time, in the religious and benevolent enterprises. They have a liberal, even an aesthetic spirit. A reference to Beauty in action sounds to be sure a little hollow and ridiculous in the ears of the old church. In politics, it has often sufficed, when they treated of justice, if they kept the bounds of selfish calculation. If they granted restitution, it was prudence which granted it. But the justice which is now claimed for the black, and the pauper, and the drunkard, is for Beauty, — is for a necessity to the soul of the agent, not of the beneficiary. I say this is the tendency, not yet the realization. Our virtue totters and trips, does not yet walk firmly. Its representatives are austere; they preach and denounce; their rectitude is not yet a grace. They are still liable to that slight taint of burlesque which in our strange world attaches to the zealot. A saint should be as dear as the apple of the eye. Yet we are tempted to smile, and we flee from the working to the speculative reformer, to escape that same slight ridicule. Alas for these days of derision and criticism! We call the Beautiful the highest, because it appears to us the golden mean, escaping the dowdiness of the good and the heartlessness of the true. They are lovers of nature also, and find an indemnity in the inviolable order of the world for the violated order and grace of man.

There is, no doubt, a great deal of well-founded objection to be spoken or felt against the sayings and doings of this class, some of whose traits we have selected; no doubt they will lay themselves open to criticism and to lampoons, and as ridiculous stories will be to be told of them as of any. There will be cant and pretension; there will be subtilty and moonshine. These persons are of unequal strength, and do not all prosper. They complain that everything around them must be denied; and if feeble, it takes all their strength to deny, before they can begin to lead their own life. Grave seniors insist on their respect to this institution and that usage; to an obsolete history; to some vocation, or college, or etiquette, or beneficiary, or charity, or morning or evening call, which they resist as what does not concern them. But it costs such sleepless nights, alienations and misgivings, — they have so many moods about it; these old guardians never change *their* minds; they have but one mood on the subject, namely, that Antony is very perverse, — that it is quite as much as Antony can do to assert his rights, abstain from what he thinks foolish, and keep his temper. He cannot help the reaction of this injustice in his own mind. He is braced-up and stilted; all freedom and flowing genius, all sallies of wit and frolic nature are quite out of the question; it is well if he can keep from lying, injustice, and suicide. This is no time for gaiety and grace. His strength and spirits are wasted in rejection. But the strong spirits overpower those around them without effort. Their thought and emotion comes in like a flood, quite withdraws them from all notice of these carping critics; they surrender themselves with glad heart to the heavenly guide, and only by implication reject the clamorous nonsense of the hour. Grave seniors talk to the deaf, — church and old book mumble and ritualize to an unheeding, preoccupied and advancing mind, and thus they by happiness of greater momentum lose no time, but take the right road at first.

But all these of whom I speak are not proficients; they are novices; they only show the road in which man should travel, when the soul has greater health and prowess. Yet let them feel the dignity of their charge, and deserve a larger power. Their heart is the ark in which the fire is concealed which shall burn in a broader and universal flame. Let them obey the Genius then most when his impulse is wildest; then most when he seems to lead to uninhabitable deserts of thought and life; for the path which the hero travels alone is the highway of health and benefit to mankind. What is the privilege and nobility of our nature but its persistency, through its power to attach itself to what is permanent?

Society also has its duties in reference to this class, and must behold them with what charity it can. Possibly some benefit may yet accrue from them to the state. In our Mechanics' Fair, there must be not only bridges, ploughs, carpenters' planes, and baking troughs, but also some few finer instruments, — rain gauges, thermometers, and telescopes; and in society, besides farmers, sailors, and weavers, there must be a few persons of purer fire kept specially as gauges and meters of character; persons of a fine, detecting instinct, who note the smallest accumulations of wit and feeling in the bystander. Perhaps too there might be room for the exciters and monitors; collectors of the heavenly spark, with power

to convey the electricity to others. Or, a the storm-tossed vessel at sea speaks the frigate or "line packet" to learn its longitude, so it may not be without its advantage that we should now and then encounter rare and gifted men, to compare the points of our spiritual compass, and verify our bearings from superior chronometers.

Amidst the downward tendency and proneness of things, when every voice is raised for a new road or another statute or a subscription of stock; for an improvement in dress, or in dentistry; for a new house or a larger business; for a political party, or the division of an estate; — will you not tolerate one or two solitary voices in the land, speaking for thoughts and principles not marketable or perishable? Soon these improvements and mechanical inventions will be superseded; these modes of living lost out of memory; these cities rotted, ruined by war, by new inventions, by new seats of trade, or the geologic changes: — all gone, like the shells which sprinkle the sea-beach with a white colony to-day, forever renewed to be forever destroyed. But the thoughts which these few hermits strove to proclaim by silence as well as by speech, not only by what they did, but by what they forebore to do, shall abide in beauty and strength, to reorganize themselves in nature, to invest themselves anew in other, perhaps higher endowed and happier mixed clay than ours, in fuller union with the surrounding system.

Ralph Waldo Emerson: ODE INSCRIBED TO W. H. CHANNING

Though loath to grieve
The evil time's sole patriot,
I cannot leave
My honied thought
For the priest's cant,
Or statesman's rant.

If I refuse
My study for their politique,
Which at the best is trick,
The angry Muse
Puts confusion in my brain.

But who is he that prates
Of the culture of mankind,
Of better arts and life?
Go, blindworm, go,
Behold the famous States
Harrying Mexico
With rifle and with knife!

Or who, with accent bolder,
Dare praise the freedom-loving mountaineer?
I found by thee, O rushing Contoocook!
And in thy valleys, Agiochook!
The jackals of the Negro-holder.

The God who made New Hampshire
Taunted the lofty land
With little men; —
Small bat and wren

House in the oak: —
If earth-fire cleave
The unheaved land, and bury the folk,
The southern crocodile would grieve.
Virtue palters; Right is hence;
Freedom praised, but hid;
Funeral eloquence
Rattles the coffin-lid.

What boots thy zeal,
O glowing friend,
That would indignant rend
The northland from the south?
Wherefore? to what good end?
Boston Bay and Bunker Hill
Would serve things still; —
Things are of the snake.

The horseman serves the horse,
The neatherd serves the neat,
The merchant serves the purse,
The eater serves his meat;
'T is the day of the chattel,
Web to weave, and corn to grind;
Things are in the saddle,
And ride mankind.

There are two laws discrete,
Not reconciled, —
Law for man, and law for thing;
The last builds town and fleet,
But it runs wild,
And doth the man unking.

'T is fit the forest fall
The steep be graded,
The mountain tunnelled,
The sand shaded,
The orchard planted,
The glebe tilled,
The prairie granted,
The steamer built.

Let man serve law for man;
Live for friendship, live for love,
For truth's and harmony's behoof;
The state may follow how it can,
As Olympus follows Jove.

Yet do not I implore
The wrinkled shopman to my sounding
    woods,
Nor bid the unwilling senator
Ask votes of thrushes in the solitudes.
Every one to his chosen work; —
Foolish hands may mix and mar;
Wise and sure the issues are.
Round they roll till dark is light,
Sex to sex, and even to odd; —
The over-god
Who marries Right to Might,
Who peoples, unpeoples, —
He who exterminates
Races by stronger races,

Black by white faces, —
Knows to bring honey
Out of the lion;
Grafts gentlest scion
On pirate and Turk.

The Cossack eats Poland,
Like stolen fruit;
Her last noble is ruined,
Her last poet mute:
Straight, into double band
The victors divide;
Half for freedom strike and stand; —
The astonished Muse finds thousands at her
    side.

James Truslow Adams: EMERSON RE-READ

EXCEPT in tales of romance it is not given to us to be able to pass through postern doors or forest glades and find ourselves in lands of leisure where it is always afternoon. If one seeks the King of Elfland's Daughter it must be between the pages of a book. Nevertheless, one can change one's stage and ways of life and amplify one's days. Some months ago by a simple shift in space I so wrought a change in time that, for a while at least, I have been able without sense of haste or pressure to browse again among the books I read and marked as a boy, books which for more years than I like to count had stood untouched upon my shelves, open apparently to the reaching hand, but in reality, owing to lack of time, as remote as boyhood's days themselves.

A week ago, I picked up one of the oldest of these, oldest in possession, not in imprint — the *Essays* of Emerson. In an unformed hand there was the inscription on the flyleaf, "James Truslow Adams, 1896." I was then seventeen, and had evidently read him earlier, for at the beginning of a number of the essays, notably "Self-Reliance," are marked the dates of reading, "1895, '96, '96, '96." The volume, one of that excellent, well-printed series which in those halcyon days the National Book Company used to sell for fifty cents, is underlined and marked with marginal notes all through. The passages are not all those I should mark to-day, but at sixteen and seventeen it is clear I was reading Emerson with great enthusiasm, and again and again.

In the past few days I have gone through five volumes of his work and found the task no light one. What, I ask myself, is the trouble? It is obviously not that Emerson is not "modern," for the other evening I read aloud, to the mutual enjoyment of my wife and myself, the *Prometheus Chained* of Æschylus, which antedates Emerson by some twenty-five hundred years. I turn to Paul More's *Shelburne Essays*, Volume XI, and read the statement that "it becomes more and more apparent that Emerson, judged by an international or even by a true national standard, is the outstanding figure of American letters."

I pause and ponder. "International," even "true national," standards are high. Whom have we? Lowell as a critic? One thinks of, say, Sainte-Beuve, and a shoulder shrug for Lowell. Lowell as poet, Whittier, Longfellow, Bryant? *Exeunt omnes,* except as second-rate by world standards. The troop of current novelists and poets are much the same here as in a half-dozen other countries. Hawthorne? A very distinctive, and yet a minor voice, in the international choir. Poe? Again a minor, and scarcely distinguishable as a "national." Whitman? One thinks of Whitman five hundred years hence in world terms, and shakes

Reprinted by permission from the *Atlantic Monthly,* 146 (October, 1930), 484-492.

one's head. The choice is narrowing fast. Is Mr. More right? Yet the Emerson who evidently so stirred me at sixteen leaves me cold to-day at fifty. It is something to be looked into. I try, at fifty, to reappraise my Emerson. I take up the volumes again to see wherein the trouble lies.

First of all it occurs to me to test him by his own appraisals of others, and I turn to his volume on *Representative Men*. The list of names is itself of considerable significance — Plato, Swedenborg, Montaigne, Shakespeare, Napoleon, Goethe. Four of these are evidently so obvious as to tell us nothing of the mind choosing them. The case is a good deal like that of the Pulitzer Jury in biography, which is forbidden to award prizes for lives of Lincoln or Washington. The essential point is, what has Emerson to say of these men?

I confess that, when after these thirty years or more I turn from reading about Emerson to reading him himself, I am rather amazed by what seems to me the shallowness of these essays. In fact, I believe that even Mr. More considers the Plato a very unsatisfactory performance. Emerson babbles of "the Franklin-like wisdom" of Socrates, and, indeed, I think we could look for as sound an essay from an intelligent undergraduate. The Shakespeare is almost equally naïve and unsatisfying, and Emerson's final judgment is that the dramatist was merely a "master of the revels to mankind," the purveyor of "very superior pyrotechny this evening," and that the end of the record must be that with all his ability he "led an obscure and a profane life, using his genius for the public amusement." This essay throws much light on Emerson if little on Shakespeare. Nor does he show more real understanding of his other

great men. He can say that Napoleon left no trace whatever on Europe, that "all passed away like the smoke of his artillery." Of Goethe's greatest poem, the *Faust*, Emerson notes mainly its "superior intelligence." One suspects that he chose these four names unconsciously because they were high in the world's record of the great, not because he understood the men or their work.

When he turns from these names, almost imposed upon him, to another of his independent choosing, it is illuminating that the one he dwells on with greatest admiration is Swedenborg. This fact is significant. For him, the Swedish mystic is "a colossal soul," the "last Father in the Church," "not likely to have a successor," compared with whom Plato is a "gownsman," whereas Lycurgus and Caesar would have to bow before the Swede. Emerson quotes from him as "golden sayings" such sentences as "in heaven the angels are advancing continually to the spring-time of their youth, so that the oldest angel appears the youngest," or "it is never permitted to any one in heaven, to stand behind another and look at the back of his head: for then the influx which is from the Lord is disturbed." Nor should we forget that entry in Emerson's *Journals* in which he noted that "for pure intellect" he had never known the equal of — Bronson Alcott!

It is true that these essays are not Emerson's best, but they were written when he was over forty years old and at the height of his fame and mental maturity, and they help us to understand our problem. They are typical products of the American mind. Conventional praise is given to the great names of Europe, with comment that indicates lack of understanding of the great currents of thought and action, while

Mrs. Eddy and Brigham Young peer over the writer's shoulders. We begin to see how deeply Emerson was an American.

His national limitation is noteworthy in another important source of influence in a mature culture, that of art. Music appears to have been outside his life and consideration. Of painting he could write that, having once really seen a great picture, there was nothing for one to gain by looking at it again. In sculpture he finds a "paltriness, as of toys and the trumpery of a theater." It "is the game of a rude and youthful people, and not the manly labor of a wise and spiritual nation," and he quotes with approval Isaac Newton's remark about "stone dolls." Art is not mature unless it is "practical and moral," and addresses the uncultivated with a "voice of lofty cheer." All art should be extempore, and he utters a genuine American note in his belief that it will somehow come to us in a new form, the religious heart raising "to a divine use the railroad, the insurance office, the joint-stock company, our law, our primary assemblies, our commerce, the galvanic battery, the electric jar, the prism, and the chemist's retort." "America is a poem in our eyes; its ample geography dazzles the imagination, and it will not wait long for metres." A century later, and we realize that something more is needful for the imagination than an ample geography.

His doctrine that art should be extempore stems from his general belief that knowledge comes from intuition rather than from thought, and that wisdom and goodness are implanted in us — a fatally easy philosophy which has always appealed to the democratic masses, and which is highly flattering to their self-esteem. Wordsworth had led the romantic reaction by making us see the beauty and value in the common things of everyday life, but the philosophy of Emerson has a different ancestry. The two when joined are a perfect soil for democratic belief, and democratic laxity in mind and spirit, far as that might be from Emerson's intention and occasional statements. The more obvious inferences are dangerous, for although a cobbler's flash of insight *may* be as great as the philosopher's lifetime of thought, such is of the rarest occurrence, and preached as a universal doctrine it is a more leveling one by far than universal suffrage.

2

As the ordinary unimportant man, such as most of us are, reads Emerson, his self-esteem begins to grow and glow. "The sweetest music is not in the oratorio, but in the human voice when it speaks from its instant tones of tenderness, truth, or courage." Culture, with us, he says, "ends in headache." "Do not craze yourself with thinking, but go about your business anywhere. Life is not intellectual or critical, but sturdy." "Why all this deference to Alfred and Scanderbeg and Gustavus? As great a stake depends on your private act to-day as followed their public and renowned steps." "We are all wise. The difference between persons is not in wisdom but in art." "Our spontaneous action is always the best. You cannot with your best deliberation and heed come so close to any question as your spontaneous glance shall bring you whilst you rise from your bed."

There is a kernel of noble thought in all this, but it is heady doctrine that may easily make men drunk and driveling, and I think we are coming near to the heart of our problem. The preaching that we do not have to think, the doctrine of what I may term, in Emerson's phrase, "the spontaneous glance," is at the bottom of that appalling refusal to criticize, analyze, ponder, which is one of the chief characteristics of the American people to-day in all its social, political, and international affairs. Many influences have united to bring about the condition, and Emerson cannot escape responsibility for being one of them.

On the other hand, a new nation, a common man with a fleeting vision of the possibility of an uncommon life, above all the youth just starting out with ambition and hope but little knowledge or influence as yet, all need the stimulation of a belief that somehow they *are* important and that not only may their private acts and lives be as high and noble as any, but that the way is open for them to make them so. This is the one fundamental American doctrine. It is the one unique contribution America has made to the common fund of civilization. Our mines and wheat fields do not differ in kind from others. With Yankee ingenuity we have seized on the ideas of others and in many cases improved their practical applications. The ideas, however, have largely come from abroad. The use of coal as fuel, the harnessing of steam and electricity for man's use, — the foundations of our era, — originated in Europe. Even the invention of the electric light was only in part American. But the doctrine of the importance of the common man is uniquely an American doctrine. It is something different, on the one hand, from the mere awarding to him of legal rights and, on the other, from the mere career open to the talents.

It is a doctrine to which the heart of humanity has responded with religious enthusiasm. It, and not science, has been the real religion of our time, and, essentially, the doctrine is a religious and not a philosophical or scientific one, equally made up as it is of a colossal hope and a colossal illusion. This does not invalidate it. Like all religions it will have its course to run and its part to play in the moulding of man to something finer. It is one more step up, and we need not deny it merely because of the inherent falsity of that gorgeous preamble which proclaims to the world, "All men are created equal." In spite of the self-assertion of the so-called masses, that is a statement which, deep in their hearts, it is as difficult for the inferior as the superior genuinely to believe. It is an ideal, which, like every religious ideal, will be of far-reaching influence, but which must be made believable emotionally. Emerson's greatness lies in his having been the greatest prophet of this new religion, an influence that might well continue to be felt on the two classes that need the doctrine most — the common man striving to rise above the mediocre, and the youth striving to attain a courageous and independent maturity.

Another strain in Emerson, that of the poet and mystic, has also to be reckoned with in making up the man's account. His insistence upon values in life, culminating in the spiritual, is one sorely needed in the America of our day as of his. We are, perhaps, further from the ideal he drew in his "American Scholar" than were the men of his own time. His large hope has not been fulfilled. There is a delicate beauty in his spiritual outlook on life, a beauty akin to that of many an old fresco in Umbria or Tuscany. Unfortunately, there were fundamental flaws in the work of the Italian artists, flaws not of spiritual insight or of artistic craftsmanship, but of wet plaster or of wrong chemical combinations in materials, so that little by little their painting has crumbled and faded. If Emerson's mysticism led him too easily toward Swedenborg rather than toward Plato, and if the beauty of his spiritual interpretation of the universe does not carry that conviction or mould his readers as it should, may we not wonder whether there were not some fundamental flaws in the mind of the man that may explain his decreasing influence, just as in examining a wall where a few patches of dim color are all that remain of a Giotto we have to consider, not the artist's love of the Madonna, but his lack of knowledge of the mechanics of his art? Of this we shall speak presently.

The quintessence of Emersonianism is to be found in the first and second series of *Essays,* and it may be noted that it was these, as my pencilings show, which I myself read most as a boy, and of them, it was such essays as "Self-Reliance," in which the word is found in its purest form, that I read over and over. What do I find marked as I turn the old pages? "Trust thyself: every heart vibrates to that iron string." "Whoso would be a man must be a nonconformist." "Nothing at last is sacred but the integrity of your own mind." "I do not wish to expiate, but to live. My life is not an apology, but a life. It is for itself and not for a spectacle." "What I must do is all that concerns me, not what the people think." "The great man is he who in the crowd keeps with perfect sweetness the independence of solitude." "Always scorn appearances and you always may. The force of character is cumulative." "Life only avails and not the having lived." "Insist on yourself; never imitate." "Nothing can bring you peace but yourself."

This is high and worthy doctrine, the practice of which will tax a man's strength and courage to the utmost, and such sentences as the above have proved the strongest influences in the making of literally countless adolescent Americans, stimulating their ambition in the noblest fashion. Unfortunately this part of Emerson's teaching has had less influence than the other. The average American soon slips into preferring "we are all wise" to "scorn appearances." Insisting on being one's self is strenuous and difficult work anywhere, more so in America than any other country I know, thanks to social opinion, mass ideals, and psychologized advertising of national products. Emerson deserves full meed of praise for preaching the value of individualism, but it may be asked, granting that nearly all intelligent, high-minded American youths for nearly a century have, at their most idealistic stage, come under the influence of Emerson's doctrine, why has the effect of his teaching been so slight upon their later manhood? Does the fault lie in them or in the great teacher, for, in such sentences as we have quoted above, I gladly allow that the sage of Concord *was* a great teacher.

The answer, I think, is that the fault lies to a great extent in Emerson himself. His doctrine contains two great flaws, one positive, the other negative, and both as typically American as he himself was in everything. That he had no logically articulated system of thought is not his weakest point. He once said that he could not give an account of himself if challenged. Attempts have been made to prove that his thought was unified and coherent. One may accept these or not. It matters little, for it is not, and never has been, as a consistent philosopher that Emerson has influenced his readers. It has been by his trenchant aphorisms which stir the soul of the young and the not too thoughtful, and set the blood to dancing like sudden strains of martial music. It is in these, and not in any metaphysical system about which philosophers might argue, that we find the fatal flaws and influences I have mentioned.

The first, the positive one, in spite of his high doctrine of self-reliance and individualism, is that Emerson makes life too easy by his insistence on intuition and spontaneity. The style and construction of his writings deliberately emphasize the import of the aphorisms. The occasionally qualifying context sinks into insignificance and out of memory as does the stick of a rocket in the darkness of night. We see and recall only the dazzling shower of stars. If this is now and then unfair to Emerson's thought, he has himself to blame. He took no pains to bind his thought together and loved the brilliancy of his rocket-stars of "sayings." We have already quoted some of these on the point we are now discussing. All teaching is "Intuition." In "Spontaneity or Instinct" he finds "the essence of genius, the essence of virtue, and the essence of life." "It is as easy for the strong man to be strong, as it is for the weak to be weak." "All good conversation, manners, and action, come from a spontaneity which forgets usages, and makes the moment great." "No man need be perplexed by his speculations. . . . These are the soul's mumps and measles and whooping-coughs." "Our moral nature is vitiated by any interference of our will. . . . There is no merit in the matter. Either God is there or he is not there. We love characters in proportion as they are impulsive and spontaneous. The less a man thinks or knows about his virtues the better we like him." A page or two back we noted his theory of spontaneity in art and intellect.

3

This, as we have said, unless the occasional qualifications are as greatly emphasized as the sayings themselves, is extremely dangerous doctrine. Of all the youths who have read Emerson in their impressionable years, a certain proportion have subsequently retrograded in the spiritual and intellectual scale, and a certain proportion have advanced. Of the difficulty with the master felt by the latter we shall speak presently, but for the first group this doctrine of spontaneity, so emphasized by Emerson, offers all too soft a cushion upon which to recline. Act and do not think. Culture is headache. Perplexities are the soul's mumps and measles. Radiant sentence after sentence, graven with clear precision on the cameo of the mind. It has been said that, of all the sages, Emerson requires the least intellectual preparation to read. He is, indeed, in some respects, and those in which he exerts most influence, fatally easy. Fatally easy and alluring to the busy hundred-per-cent American is this doctrine of intuition and spontaneity. It is a siren voice, a soft Lydian air blown across the blue water of the mind's tropical sea. For a century the American has left the plain hard work of life to his foreign serfs. The backbreaking toil of digging trenches, laying rails, puddling iron in the furnaces, has been delegated successively to the Irish, the Italians, the Slavs. But thinking is intellectually, willing is spiritually, as backbreaking as these. The ordinary American prefers also to abandon them and to take for himself the easier task of solving the economic problems and puzzles in which he delights. Intuition and spontaneity — fatal words for a civilization which is more and more coming to depend for its very existence on clear, hard, and long-sustained "thinking-through." It is this positive flaw in Emerson's teaching that has made the effect of his really noble doctrines of so little influence upon the boys who have worshiped him this side idolatry at sixteen and then gone into the world and found every invitation to retreat from the high ground rather than to advance.

What now of those others, those who also worshiped Emerson in youth, who have fought the world, and who find him declining in influence over their lives the more they advance? With them we reach Emerson's negative flaw.

What a gulf between the man of fifty and the boy of sixteen! As one has in those intervening years studied the history of the past, watched the daily life of the people of a score of nations, seen wars and famines take their toll of millions, and, nearer one's own heart, watched the physical pain of those closest to one's self, stood at grave after grave, found, too, perhaps, that one has wrought evil when most striving to do good, one has come to feel the whole mystery of that problem of Evil — of sin, of suffering, of death. One may yet carry a brave heart and hold one's self erect, but one is no longer content with a philosophy of shallow optimism, a "God's in his heaven — all's right with the world."

I think that here is where Emerson fails us as we grow older and wiser. The trumpet blasts of self-reliance which so thrilled us at sixteen sound a little thin and far-off now. We needed them when they first smote our ear and we are deeply grateful, but we have fought the fight, we have tried to be ourselves, we have tried to live our life for itself and not for a spectacle, and now we are older. We have lived, loved, suffered, enjoyed, fought, and to some extent won. The world has been rich in interest — and in suffering. There are hopeful signs on every side. There is sunlight as well as darkness, but there *is* darkness. One has been close to failure and looked it in the eye. There have been the brows we could not soothe through years of suffering,

the waxen faces we kissed for the last time before we laid them away, the mysterious darkness coming toward ourselves like the shadow of a cloud on a summer landscape, but inevitably to overtake us. When we turn again to the great teacher of our youth, what does he say to help or hearten us? Nothing.

Owing largely to material circumstance and a vast and uninhabited continent, the prevailing mood of the American people came to be one of shallow and unlimited optimism, the waves of which flowed over even the sectional Calvinism of New England. Nature ceased to be the evil enemy of man's spirit and gave him her fairest gifts, as Mephistopheles bestowed his Helen on the tortured Faust. With material abundance, spiritual evil ceased to appear important and a golden age seemed dawning, as youth came to Faust in that most un-American legend.

For its hundred and fifty years America has been scarcely touched by suffering. Pestilence? None. Think of the Black Death and other great plagues that have swept over Europe. Famine? None. Think of India and China. War? Scarcely more than one. In the Revolution only an infinitesimal part of the population was in the army for any length of time. The War of 1812 was a ripple, almost all at sea, and the deaths were negligible to the population. The Indian Wars? Skirmishes by paid troops. The Mexican War? A junket which never came home to the people. The Civil War? Yes, but even that did not come home to the whole civilian population, except in the South, as have the wars which have flowed in torrents over Europe. Compare it with the Thirty Years' War, in which, to say nothing of the rest of Europe, the population of Germany, from the ravages of the sword, famine, disease, and emigration, sank from 16,000,000 to 6,000,000, and in which of 35,000 villages in Bohemia less than 6000 were standing at the end, and in which nine tenths of the entire population of the Palatinate disappeared. The Spanish War was a holiday affair except for a few homes. In the last Great War we lost by death a mere 126,000 as compared with 8,500,000 in the Old World. In civil life our history has been one long business boom, punctuated by an occasional panic, like a fit of indigestion for a man who continually overeats. We have never suffered like the rest of humanity, and have waxed fat without, as yet, having to consider the problems forced upon others, until we have ceased to believe in their reality. The dominant American note has thus been one of a buoyant and unthinking optimism. America is a child who has never gazed on the face of death.

Emerson somewhere speaks of "the nonchalance of boys sure of a dinner." Can any words better express the American attitude toward the universe, and, in spite of his spirituality and the somewhat faded fresco of his mysticism, does Emerson himself really give us anything deeper? Man, according to him, "is born to be rich." Economic evils trouble our sage not at all. The universe, for him, is good through and through, and "success consists in close application to the laws of the world, and, since those laws are intellectual and moral, an intellectual and moral obedience." One thinks of Jay Gould and the career of many a magnate of to-day! "In a free and just commonwealth, property rushes from the idle and imbecile, to the industrious, brave, and persevering." As I am certainly not idle (I am working on a holiday to write this), and as Americans would not admit that theirs is not a just and free commonwealth, imbecility is the only third horn of the trilemma on which to impale myself if property has not rushed toward me. "Do not skulk," the sage tells every man in "a world which exists for him." At fifty, we have found, simply, that the world does *not* exist for us. "Love and you shall be loved. All love is mathematically just, as much as the two sides of an algebraic problem." One rubs one's eyes. "There is a soul at the center of nature and over the will of every man, so that none of us can wrong the universe." Man may, he says, "easily dismiss all particular uncertainties and fears, and adjourn to the sure revelation of time the solution of his private riddles. He is sure his welfare is dear to the heart of being." Is he so sure? Alas, no longer.

4

As I think over my most recent visit to Rome, where two thousand years of human history, happiness, and suffering have left their monuments, and Heaven knows how many thousand unmarked before, I contrast it with a visit to Emerson's house at Concord on an October day many years ago. It is a charming, roomy old house, and in it Emerson was able to live with a large library and three servants on two thousand a year. In the ineffable light of an American autumn, as I saw it, it was a place of infinite peace. Concord in 1840 was an idyllic moment in the history of the race. That moment came and passed, like a baby's smile. Emerson lived in it. "In the morning," he wrote, "I awake, and find the old world, wife, babes, and mother, Concord and Boston, the dear old spiritual world, and even the dear old devil not far off."

It is true that he has very occasional qualms and doubts. He even wonders in one essay whether we must presuppose some "slight treachery and derision" in the universe. As we turn the pages, we ask ourselves with some impatience, "Did

is man never really suffer?" and read
at "the only thing grief has taught me,
to know how shallow it is. That, like
ll the rest, plays about the surface, and
ever introduces me into the reality, for
ontact with which, we would even pay
he costly price of sons and lovers."

One ends. Perhaps Mr. More is right.
Perhaps Emerson *is* the outstanding fig-
re in American letters. Who else has
xpressed so magnificently the hope, and
o tragically illustrated the illusion, of
ur unique contribution to the world?
My own debt to the sage is unpayable.
He was one of the great influences in my
early life, as, in his highest teaching, he
hould be in that of every boy. It seems
lmost the basest of treason to write this
essay, and I would still have every youth
ead his Emerson. But what of America?
What of the hope and the illusion? A
century has passed. Is no one to arise
who will fuse them both in some larger
synthesis, and who, inspiring youth, will
not be a broken reed in maturity? Are
our letters and philosophy to remain the
child until the Gorgon faces of evil, dis-
aster, and death freeze our own unlined
ones into eternal stone? Is it well that
the outstanding figure in American letters should be one whose influence di-
minishes in proportion as the minds of
his readers grow in strength, breadth,
and maturity? And, speaking generally,
is this not true of Emerson? Does any
man of steadily growing character,
wealth of experience, and strength of
mind find the significance and influence
of Emerson for him growing as the years
pass? Does he turn to him more and
more for counsel, help, or solace?

There is but one answer, I think, and
that is negative. Unlike the truly great,
the influence of Emerson shrinks for most
of us as we ourselves develop. May the
cause not lie in the two flaws I have
pointed out, flaws in the man as in his

doctrine in spite of the serene nobility
of so much of his life? If with all his
wide and infinitely varied reading, noted
in his *Journals,* we find his culture a bit
thin and puerile, is it not because he himself trusted too much to that theory of
spontaneity, of the "spontaneous glance,"
rather than to the harder processes of
scholarship and thinking-through coherently; and if we find him lacking in
depth and virility, is it not because he
allowed himself to become a victim to
that vast American optimism with its
refusal to recognize and wrestle with the
problem of evil? One turns to Æschylus
and reads: —

. . . affliction knows no rest,
But rolls from breast to breast its vagrant tide.

One does not need to be a pessimist,
merely human, to find here the deeper
and more authentic note.

If Emerson is still the outstanding figure in American letters, is that not the
equivalent of saying that America a century after the *Essays* appeared has not
yet grown to mental maturity, and that
the gospel it preaches is inspiring only
for unformed adolescence, — of whatever
age, — without having risen to a compre-
hension of the problems of maturity? In
Europe, the past has bequeathed not
only a wealth of art, but a legacy of evil
borne and sorrow felt. Perhaps American
letters, like American men, will not grow
beyond the simple optimism and, in one
aspect, the shallow doctrine of Emerson
until they too shall have suffered and
sorrowed. Emerson, in his weakness as
in his strength, is American through and
through. He could have been the product, in his entirety, of no other land, and
that land will not outgrow him until it
has some day passed through the fires of
a suffering unfelt by him and as yet
escaped by it.

Henry David Thoreau: CIVIL DISOBEDIENCE

I HEARTILY accept the motto, — "That government is best which governs least"; and I should like to see it acted up to more rapidly and systematically. Carried out, it finally amounts to this, which also I believe, — "That government is best which governs not at all"; and when men are prepared for it, that will be the kind of government which they will have. Government is at best but an expedient; but most governments are usually, and all governments are sometimes, inexpedient. The objections which have been brought against a standing army, and they are many and weighty, and deserve to prevail, may also at last be brought against a standing government. The standing army is only an arm of the standing government. The government itself, which is only the mode which the people have chosen to execute their will, is equally liable to be abused and perverted before the people can act through it. Witness the present Mexican war, the work of comparatively a few individuals using the standing government as their tool; for, in the outset, the people would not have consented to this measure.

This American government, — what is it but a tradition, though a recent one, endeavoring to transmit itself unimpaired to posterity, but each instant losing some of its integrity? It has not the vitality and force of a single living man; for a single man can bend it to his will. It is a sort of wooden gun to the people themselves. But it is not the less necessary for this; for the people must have some complicated machinery or other, and hear its din, to satisfy that idea of government which they have. Governments show thus how successfully men can be imposed on, even impose on themselves, for their own advantage. It is excellent, we must all allow. Yet this government never of itself furthered any enterprise, but by the alacrity with which it got out of its way. It does not keep the country free. It does not settle the West. It does not educate. The character inherent in the American people has done all that has been accomplished; and it would have done somewhat more, if the government had not sometimes got in its way. For government is an expedient by which men would fain succeed in letting one another alone; and, as has been said, when it is most expedient, the governed are most let alone by it. Trade and commerce, if they were not made of India-rubber, would never manage to bounce over the obstacles which legislators are continually putting in their way; and, if one were to judge these men wholly by the effects of their actions and not partly by their intentions, they would deserve to be classed and punished with those mischievous persons who put obstructions on the railroads.

But, to speak practically and as a citizen, unlike those who call themselves no-government men, I ask for, not at once no government, but at once a better government. Let every man make known what kind of government would command his respect, and that will be one step toward obtaining it.

After all, the practical reason why, when the power is once in the hands of the people, a majority are permitted, and for a long period continue, to rule is not because they are most likely to be in the right, nor because this seems fairest to the minority, but because they are physically the strongest. But a government in which the majority rule in all cases cannot be based on justice, even as far as men understand it. Can there not be a government in which majorities do not virtually decide right and wrong, but conscience? — in which majorities decide only those questions to which the rule of expediency is applicable? Must the citizen ever for a moment, or in the least degree, resign his conscience to the legislator? Why has every man a conscience, then? I think that we should be men first, and subjects afterward. It is not desirable to cultivate a respect for the law, so much as for the right. The only obligation which I have a right to assume is to do at any time what I think right. It is truly enough said, that a corporation has no conscience; but a corporation of conscientious men is a corporation *with* a conscience. Law never made men a whit more just; and, by means of their respect for it, even the well-disposed are daily made the agents of injustice. A common and natural result of an undue respect for law is, that you may see a file of soldiers, colonel, captain, corporal, privates, powder-monkeys, and all, marching in admirable order over hill and dale to the wars, against their wills, ay, against their common sense and consciences, which makes it very steep marching indeed, and produces a palpitation of the heart. They have no doubt that it is a damnable business in which they are concerned; they are all peaceably inclined. Now, what are they? Men at all? or small movable forts and magazines, at the service of some unscrupulous man in power? Visit the Navy-Yard, and behold a marine, such a man as an American government can make, or such as it can make a man with its black arts, — a mere shadow and reminiscence of humanity, a man laid out alive and standing, and already, as one may say, buried under arms with funeral accompaniments, though it may be, —

Not a drum was heard, not a funeral note,
  As his corse to the rampart we hurried;
Not a soldier discharged his farewell shot
  O'er the grave where our hero we buried.

The mass of men serve the state thus, not as men mainly, but as machines, with their bodies. They are the standing army, and the militia, jailers, constables, posse comitatus, etc. In most cases there is no free exercise whatever of the judgment or of the moral sense; but they put themselves on a level with wood and earth and stones; and wooden men can perhaps be manufactured that will serve the purpose as well. Such command no more respect than men of straw or a lump of dirt. They have the same sort of worth only as horses and dogs. Yet such as these even are commonly esteemed good citizens. Others — as most legislators, politicians, lawyers, ministers, and officeholders — serve the state chiefly with their heads; and, as they rarely make any moral distinctions, they are as likely to serve the Devil, without *intending* it, as God. A very few, as heroes, patriots, martyrs, reformers in the great sense, and *men*, serve the state with their consciences also, and so necessarily resist it for the most part; and they are commonly treated as enemies by it. A wise man will only be useful as a man, and will not submit to be "clay," and "stop a hole to keep the wind away," but leave that office to his dust at least:

I am too high-born to be propertied,
To be a secondary at control,
Or useful serving-man and instrument
To any sovereign state throughout the world.

He who gives himself entirely to his fellow-men appears to them useless and selfish; but he who gives himself partially to them is pronounced a benefactor and philanthropist.

How does it become a man to behave toward this American government to-day? I answer, that he cannot without disgrace be associated with it. I cannot for an instant recognize that political organization as *my* government which is the *slave's* government also.

All men recognize the right of revolution; that is, the right to refuse allegiance to, and to resist, the government, when its tyranny or its inefficiency are great and unendurable. But almost all say that such is not the case now. But such was the case, they think, in the Revolution of '75. If one were to tell me that this was a bad government because it taxed certain foreign commodities brought to its ports, it is most probable that I should not make an ado about it, for I can do without them. All machines have their friction; and possibly this does enough good to counterbalance the evil. At any rate, it is a great evil to make a stir about it. But when the friction comes to have its machine, and oppression and robbery are organized, I say, let us not have such a machine any longer. In other

words, when a sixth of the population of a nation which has undertaken to be the refuge of liberty are slaves, and a whole country is unjustly overrun and conquered by a foreign army, and subjected to military law, I think that it is not too soon for honest men to rebel and revolutionize. What makes this duty the more urgent is the fact that the country so overrun is not our own, but ours is the invading army.

Paley, a common authority with many on moral questions, in his chapter on the "Duty of Submission to Civil Government," resolves all civil obligation into expediency; and he proceeds to say, "that so long as the interest of the whole society requires it, that is, so long as the established government cannot be resisted or changed without public inconveniency, it is the will of God that the established government be obeyed, and no longer. . . . This principle being admitted, the justice of every particular case of resistance is reduced to a computation of the quantity of the danger and grievance on the one side, and of the probability and expense of redressing it on the other." Of this, he says, every man shall judge for himself. But Paley appears never to have contemplated those cases to which the rule of expediency does not apply, in which a people, as well as an individual, must do justice, cost what it may. If I have unjustly wrested a plank from a drowning man, I must restore it to him though I drown myself. This, according to Paley, would be inconvenient. But he that would save his life, in such a case, shall lose it. This people must cease to hold slaves, and to make war on Mexico, though it cost them their existence as a people.

In their practice, nations agree with Paley; but does any one think that Mass sachusetts does exactly what is right at the present crisis?

A drab of state, a cloth-o'-silver slut,
To have her train borne up, and her soul trail in the dirt.

Practically speaking, the opponents to a reform in Massachusetts are not a hundred thousand politicians at the South, but a hundred thousand merchants and farmers here, who are more interested in commerce and agriculture than they are in humanity, and are not prepared to do justice to the slave and to Mexico, *cost what it may.* I quarrel not with far-off foes, but with those who, near at home, cooperate with, and do the bidding of, those far away, and without whom the latter would be harmless. We are accustomed to say, that the mass of men are unprepared; but improvement is slow, because the few are not materially wiser or better than the many. It is not so important that many should be as good as you, as that there be some absolute goodness somewhere; for that will leaven the whole lump. There are thousands who are *in opinion* opposed to slavery and to the war, who yet in effect do nothing to put an end to them; who, esteeming themselves children of Washington and Franklin, sit down with their hands in their pockets, and say that they know not what to do, and do nothing; who even postpone the question of freedom to the question of free-trade, and quietly read the prices-current along with the latest advices from Mexico, after dinner, and, it may be, fall asleep over them both. What is the price-current of an honest man and patriot to-day? They hesitate, and they regret, and sometimes they petition; but they do nothing in earnest and with effect. They will wait, well disposed, for others to remedy the evil, that they may no longer have it to regret. At most, they give only a cheap vote, and a feeble countenance and Godspeed, to the right, as it goes by them. There are nine hundred and ninety-nine patrons of virtue to one virtuous man. But it is easier to deal with the real possessor of a thing than with the temporary guardian of it.

All voting is a sort of gaming, like checkers or backgammon, with a slight moral tinge to it, a playing with right and wrong, with moral questions; and betting naturally accompanies it. The character of the voters is not staked. I cast my vote, perchance, as I think right; but I am not vitally concerned that that right should prevail. I am willing to leave it to the majority. Its obligation, therefore, never exceeds that of expediency. Even voting *for the right* is *doing* nothing for it. It is only expressing to men feebly your desire that it should prevail. A wise man will not leave the right to the mercy of chance, nor wish it to prevail through the power of majority. There is but little virtue in the action of masses of men. When the majority shall at length vote for the abolition of slavery, it will be because they are indifferent to slavery, or because there is but little slavery left to be abolished by their vote. *They* will then be the only slaves. Only *his* vote can hasten the abolition of slavery who asserts his own freedom by his vote.

I hear of a convention to be held at Baltimore, or elsewhere, for the selection of a candidate for the Presidency, made up chiefly of editors, and men who are politicians by profession; but I think, what is it to any independent, intelligent, and respectable man what decision they may come to? Shall we not have the advantage of his wisdom and honesty, nevertheless? Can we not count upon some independent votes? Are there not many individuals in the country who do not attend conventions? But no: I find that the respectable man, so called, has immediately drifted from his position, and despairs of his country, when his country has more reason to despair of him. He forthwith adopts one of the candidates thus selected as the only *available* one, thus proving that he is himself *available* for any purposes of the demagogue. His vote is of no more worth than that of any unprincipled foreigner or hireling native, who may have been bought. O for a man who is a *man*, and, as my neighbor says, has a bone in his back which you cannot pass your hand through! Our statistics are at fault: the population has been returned too large. How many *men* are there to a square thousand miles in this country? Hardly one. Does not America offer any inducement for men to settle here? The American has dwindled into an Odd Fellow, — one who may be known by the development of his organ of gregariousness, and a manifest lack of intellect and cheerful self-reliance; whose first and chief concern, on coming into the world, is to see that the Alms-houses are in good repair; and, before yet he has lawfully donned the virile garb, to collect a fund for the support of the widows and orphans that may be; who, in short, ventures to live only by the aid of the Mutual Insurance company, which has promised to bury him decently.

It is not a man's duty, as a matter of course, to devote himself to the eradication of any, even the most enormous wrong; he may still properly have other concerns to engage him; but it is his duty, at least, to wash his hands of it, and, if he gives it no thought longer, not to give it practically his support. If I devote myself to other pursuits and contemplations, I must first see, at least, that I do not pursue them sitting upon another man's shoulders. I must get off him first, that he may pursue his contemplations too. See what gross inconsistency is tolerated. I have heard some of my townsmen say, "I should like to have them order me out to help put down an insurrection of the slaves, or to march to Mexico; — see if I would go"; and yet these very men have each, directly by their allegiance, and so indirectly, at least, by their money, furnished a substitute. The soldier is applauded who refuses to serve in an unjust war by those who do not refuse to sustain the unjust government which makes the war; is applauded by those whose own act and authority he disregards and sets at naught; as if the state were penitent to that degree that it hired one to scourge it while it sinned, but not to that degree that it left off sinning for a moment. Thus, under the name of Order and Civil Government, we are all made at last to pay homage to and support our own meanness. After the first blush of sin comes its indifference; and from immoral it becomes, as it were, *un*moral, and not quite unnecessary to that life which we have made.

The broadest and most prevalent error requires the most disinterested virtue to sustain it. The slight reproach to which the virtue of patriotism is commonly liable, the noble are most likely to incur. Those who, while they disapprove of the character and measures of a government, yield to it their allegiance and support are undoubtedly its most conscientious supporters, and so frequently the most serious obstacles to reform. Some are petitioning the state to dissolve the Union, to disregard the requisitions of the President. Why do they not dissolve

t themselves, — the union between them-
elves and the state, — and refuse to pay
their quota into its treasury? Do not they
stand in the same relation to the state
that the state does to the Union? And
have not the same reasons prevented the
state from resisting the Union which
have prevented them from resisting the
state?

How can a man be satisfied to entertain an opinion merely, and enjoy *it*? Is
there any enjoyment in it, if his opinion
is that he is aggrieved? If you are cheated
out of a single dollar by your neighbor,
you do not rest satisfied with knowing
that you are cheated, or with saying that
you are cheated, or even with petitioning
him to pay you your due; but you take
effectual steps at once to obtain the full
amount, and see that you are never
cheated again. Action from principle, the
perception and the performance of right,
changes things and relations; it is essentially revolutionary, and does not consist
wholly with anything which was. It not
only divides states and churches, it divides families; ay, it divides the *individual,* separating the diabolical in him
from the divine.

Unjust laws exist: shall we be content
to obey them, or shall we endeavor to
amend them, and obey them until we
have succeeded, or shall we transgress
them at once? Men generally, under
such a government as this, think that
they ought to wait until they have persuaded the majority to alter them. They
think that, if they should resist, the
remedy would be worse than the evil.
But it is the fault of the government itself that the remedy *is* worse than the
evil. *It* makes it worse. Why is it not
more apt to anticipate and provide for
reform? Why does it not cherish its wise
minority? Why does it cry and resist before it is hurt? Why does it not encour-

age its citizens to be on the alert to point
out its faults, and *do* better than it would
have them? Why does it always crucify
Christ, and excommunicate Copernicus
and Luther, and pronounce Washington
and Franklin rebels?

One would think, that a deliberate and
practical denial of its authority was the
only offense never contemplated by government; else, why has it not assigned
its definite, its suitable and proportionate
penalty? If a man who has no property
refuses but once to earn nine shillings
for the state, he is put in prison for a
period unlimited by any law that I know,
and determined only by the discretion
of those who placed him there; but if he
should steal ninety times nine shillings
from the state, he is soon permitted to
go at large again.

If the injustice is part of the necessary
friction of the machine of government,
let it go, let it go: perchance it will wear
smooth, — certainly the machine will wear
out. If the injustice has a spring, or a
pulley, or a rope, or a crank, exclusively
for itself, then perhaps you may consider
whether the remedy will not be worse
than the evil; but if it is of such a nature
that it requires you to be the agent of injustice to another, then, I say, break the
law. Let your life be a counter friction to
stop the machine. What I have to do is to
see, at any rate, that I do not lend myself
to the wrong which I condemn.

As for adopting the ways which the
state has provided for remedying the
evil, I know not of such ways. They take
too much time, and a man's life will be
gone. I have other affairs to attend to.
I came into this world, not chiefly to
make this a good place to live in, but to
live in it, be it good or bad. A man has
not everything to do, but something; and
because he cannot do *everything*, it is not
necessary that he should do *something*

wrong. It is not my business to be petitioning the Governor or the Legislature any more than it is theirs to petition me; and if they should not hear my petition, what should I do then? But in this case the state has provided no way: its very Constitution is the evil. This may seem to be harsh and stubborn and unconciliatory; but it is to treat with the utmost kindness and consideration the only spirit that can appreciate or deserves it. So is all change for the better, like birth and death, which convulse the body.

I do not hesitate to say, that those who call themselves Abolitionists should at once effectually withdraw their support, both in person and property, from the government of Massachusetts, and not wait till they constitute a majority of one, before they suffer the right to prevail through them. I think that it is enough if they have God on their side, without waiting for that other one. Moreover, any man more right than his neighbors constitutes a majority of one already.

I meet this American government, or its representative, the state government, directly, and face to face, once a year — no more — in the person of its tax-gatherer; this is the only mode in which a man situated as I am necessarily meets it; and it then says distinctly, Recognize me; and the simplest, the most effectual, and, in the present posture of affairs, the indispensablest mode of treating with it on this head, of expressing your little satisfaction with and love for it, is to deny it then. My civil neighbor, the tax-gatherer, is the very man I have to deal with, — for it is, after all, with men and not with parchment that I quarrel, — and he has voluntarily chosen to be an agent of the government. How shall he ever know well what he is and does as an officer of the government, or as a man, until he is obliged to consider whether he shall treat me, his neighbor, for whom he has respect, as a neighbor and well-disposed man, or as a maniac and disturber of the peace, and see if he can get over this obstruction to his neighborliness without a ruder and more impetuous thought or speech corresponding with his action. I know this well, that if one thousand, if one hundred, if ten men whom I could name, — if ten honest men only, — ay, if one HONEST man, in this State of Massachusetts, ceasing to hold slaves, were actually to withdraw from this copartnership, and be locked up in the county jail therefor, it would be the abolition of slavery in America. For it matters not how small the beginning may seem to be: what is once well done is done forever. But we love better to talk about it: that we say is our mission. Reform keeps many scores of newspapers in its service, but not one man. If my esteemed neighbor, the State's ambassador, who will devote his days to the settlement of the question of human rights in the Council Chamber, instead of being threatened with the prisons of Carolina, were to sit down the prisoner of Massachusetts, that State which is so anxious to foist the sin of slavery upon her sister, — though at present she can discover only an act of inhospitality to be the ground of a quarrel with her, — the Legislature would not wholly waive the subject the following winter.

Under a government which imprisons any unjustly, the true place for a just man is also a prison. The proper place to-day, the only place which Massachusetts has provided for her free and less desponding spirit, is in her prisons, to be put out and locked out of the State by her own act, as they have already put themselves out by their principles. It is there that the fugitive slave, and the Mexican prisoner on parole, and the Indian come to plead the wrongs of his race should find them; on that separate, but more free and honorable ground, where the State places those who are not *with* her, but *against* her, — the only house in a slave State in which a free man can abide with honor. If any think that their influence would be lost there, and their voices no longer afflict the ear of the State, that they would not be as an enemy within its walls, they do not know by how much truth is stronger than error, nor how much more eloquently and effectively he can combat injustice who has experienced a little in his own person. Cast your whole vote, not a strip of paper merely, but your whole influence. A minority is powerless while it conforms to the majority; it is not even a minority then; but it is irresistible when it clogs by its whole weight. If the alternative is to keep all just men in prison, or give up war and slavery, the State will not hesitate which to choose. If a thousand men were not to pay their tax-bills this year, that would not be a violent and bloody measure, as it would be to pay them, and enable the State to commit violence and shed innocent blood. This is, in fact, the definition of a peaceable revolution, if any such is possible. If the tax-gatherer, or any other public officer, asks me, as one has done, "But what shall I do?" my answer is, "If you really wish to do anything, resign your office." When the subject has refused allegiance, and the officer has resigned his office, then the revolution is accomplished. But even suppose blood should flow. Is there not a sort of blood shed when the conscience is wounded? Through this wound a man's real manhood and immortality flow out, and he bleeds to an everlasting death. I see this blood flowing now.

I have contemplated the imprisonment of the offender, rather than the seizure of his goods, — though both will serve the same purpose, — because they who assert the purest right, and consequently are most dangerous to a corrupt State, commonly have not spent much time in accumulating property. To such the State renders comparatively small service, and a slight tax is wont to appear exorbitant, particularly if they are obliged to earn it by special labor with their hands. If there were one who lived wholly without the use of money, the State itself would hesitate to demand it of him. But the rich man — not to make any invidious comparison — is always sold to the institution which makes him rich. Absolutely speaking, the more money, the less virtue; for money comes between a man and his objects, and obtains them for him; and it was certainly no great virtue to obtain it. It puts to rest many questions which he would otherwise be taxed to answer; while the only new question which it puts is the hard but superfluous one, how to spend it. Thus his moral ground is taken from under his feet. The opportunities of living are diminished in proportion as what are called the "means" are increased. The best thing a man can do for his culture when he is rich is to endeavor to carry out those schemes which he entertained when he was poor. Christ answered the Herodians according to their condition. "Show me the tribute-money," said he; — and one took a penny out of his pocket; — if you use money which has the image of Caesar on it, and which he has made current and valuable, that is, *if you are men of the State*, and gladly enjoy the advantages of Caesar's government, then pay him back some of his own when he demands it. "Render therefore to Caesar that which is Caesar's, and to God those things which are God's," — leaving them no wiser than before as to which was which; for they did not wish to know.

When I converse with the freest of my neighbors, I perceive that, whatever they may say about the magnitude and seriousness of the question, and their regard for the public tranquillity, the long and short of the matter is, that they cannot spare the protection of the existing government, and they dread the consequences to their property and families of disobedience to it. For my own part, I should not like to think that I ever rely on the protection of the State. But, if I deny the authority of the State when it presents its tax-bill, it will soon take and waste all my property, and so harass me and my children without end. This is hard. This makes it impossible for a man to live honestly, and at the same time comfortably, in outward respects. It will not be worth the while to accumulate property; that would be sure to go again. You must hire or squat somewhere, and raise but a small crop, and eat that soon. You must live within yourself, and depend upon yourself always tucked up and ready for a start, and not have many affairs. A man may grow rich in Turkey even, if he will be in all respects a good subject of the Turkish government. Confucius said: "If a state is governed by the principles of reason, poverty and misery are subjects of shame; if a state is not governed by the principles of reason, riches and honors are the subjects of shame." No: until I want the protection of Massachusetts to be extended to me in some distant Southern port, where my liberty is endangered, or until I am bent solely on building up an estate at home by peaceful enterprise, I can afford to refuse allegiance to Massachusetts, and her right to my property and life. It costs me less in every sense to incur the penalty of disobedience to the State than it would to obey. I should feel as if I were worth less in that case.

Some years ago, the State met me in behalf of the Church, and commanded me to pay a certain sum toward the support of a clergyman whose preaching my father attended, but never I myself. "Pay," it said, "or be locked up in the jail." I declined to pay. But, unfortunately, another man saw fit to pay it. I did not see why the schoolmaster should be taxed to support the priest, and not the priest the schoolmaster; for I was not the State's schoolmaster, but I supported myself by voluntary subscription. I did not see why the lyceum should not present its tax-bill, and have the State to back its demand, as well as the Church. However, at the request of the selectmen, I condescended to make some such statement as this in writing: — "Know all men by these presents, that I, Henry Thoreau, do not wish to be regarded as a member of any incorporated society which I have not joined." This I gave to the town clerk; and he has it. The State, having thus learned that I did not wish to be regarded as a member of that church, has never made a like demand on me since; though it said that it must adhere to its original presumption that time. If I had known how to name them, I should then have signed off in detail from all the societies which I never signed onto; but I did not know where to find a complete list.

I have paid no poll-tax for six years. I was put into a jail once on this account, for one night; and, as I stood considering the walls of solid stone, two or three feet thick, the door of wood and iron, a foot thick, and the iron grating which strained the light, I could not help being struck with the foolishness of that institution which treated me as if I were mere flesh and blood and bones, to be locked up. I wondered that it should have concluded at length that this was the best use it could put me to, and had never thought to avail itself of my services in some way. I saw that, if there was a wall of stone between me and my townsmen, there was a still more difficult one to climb or break through before they could get to be as free as I was. I did not for a moment feel confined, and the walls seemed a great waste of stone and mortar. I felt as if I alone of all my townsmen had paid my tax. They plainly did not know how to treat me, but behaved like persons who are underbred. In every threat and in every compliment there was a blunder; for they thought that my chief desire was to stand the other side of that stone wall. I could not but smile to see how industriously they locked the door on my meditations, which followed them out again without let or hindrance, and *they* were really all that was dangerous. As they could not reach me, they had resolved to punish my body; just as boys, if they cannot come at some person against whom they have a spite, will abuse his dog. I saw that the State was half-witted, that it was timid as a lone woman with her silver spoons, and that it did not know its friends from its foes, and I lost all my remaining respect for it, and pitied it.

Thus the State never intentionally confronts a man's sense, intellectual or moral, but only his body, his senses. It is not armed with superior wit or honesty, but with superior physical strength. I was not born to be forced. I will breathe after my own fashion. Let us see who is the strongest. What force has a multitude? They only can force me who obey a higher law than I. They force me to become like themselves. I do not hear of *men* being *forced* to live this way or that by masses of men. What sort of life were that to live? When I meet a government which says to me, "Your money or your life," why should I be in haste to give it my money? It may be in a great strait, and not know what to do: I cannot

help that. It must help itself; do as I do. It is not worth the while to snivel about it. I am not responsible for the successful working of the machinery of society. I am not the son of the engineer. I perceive that, when an acorn and a chestnut fall side by side, the one does not remain inert to make way for the other, but both obey their own laws, and spring and grow and flourish as best they can, till one, perchance, overshadows and destroys the other. If a plant cannot live according to its nature, it dies; and so a man.

The night in prison was novel and interesting enough. The prisoners in their shirt-sleeves were enjoying a chat and the evening air in the doorway, when I entered. But the jailer said, "Come, boys, it is time to lock up"; and so they dispersed, and I heard the sound of their steps returning into the hollow apartments. My roommate was introduced to me by the jailer as "a first-rate fellow and a clever man." When the door was locked, he showed me where to hang my hat, and how he managed matters there. The rooms were whitewashed once a month; and this one, at least, was the whitest, most simply furnished, and probably the neatest apartment in the town. He naturally wanted to know where I came from, and what brought me there; and, when I had told him, I asked him in my turn how he came there, presuming him to be an honest man, of course; and, as the world goes, I believe he was. "Why," said he, "they accuse me of burning a barn; but I never did it." As near as I could discover, he had probably gone to bed in a barn when drunk, and smoked his pipe there; and so a barn was burnt. He had the reputation of being a clever man, had been there some three months waiting for his trial to come on, and would have to wait as much longer; but he was quite domesticated and contented, since he got his board for nothing, and thought that he was well treated.

He occupied one window, and I the other; and I saw that if one stayed there long, his principal business would be to look out the window. I had soon read all the tracts that were left there, and examined where former prisoners had broken out, and where a grate had been sawed off, and heard the history of the various occupants of that room; for I found that even here there was a history and a gossip which never circulated beyond the walls of the jail. Probably this is the only house in the town where verses are composed, which are afterward printed in a circular form, but not published. I was shown quite a long list of verses which were composed by some young men who had been detected in an attempt to escape, who avenged themselves by singing them.

I pumped my fellow-prisoner as dry as I could, for fear I should never see him again; but at length he showed me which was my bed, and left me to blow out the lamp.

It was like traveling into a far country, such as I had never expected to behold, to lie there for one night. It seemed to me that I never had heard the town-clock strike before, nor the evening sounds of the village; for we slept with the windows open, which were inside the grating. It was to see my native village in the light of the Middle Ages, and our Concord was turned into a Rhine stream, and visions of knights and castles passed before me. They were the voices of old burghers that I heard in the streets. I was an involuntary spectator and auditor of whatever was done and said in the kitchen of the adjacent village-inn, — a wholly new and rare experience to me.

It was a closer view of my native town. I was fairly inside of it. I never had seen its institutions before. This is one of its peculiar institutions; for it is a shire town. I began to comprehend what its inhabitants were about.

In the morning, our breakfasts were put through the hole in the door, in small oblong-square tin pans, made to fit, and holding a pint of chocolate, with brown bread, and an iron spoon. When they called for the vessels again, I was green enough to return what bread I had left; but my comrade seized it, and said that I should lay that up for lunch or dinner. Soon after he was let out to work at haying in a neighboring field, whither he went every day, and would not be back till noon; so he bade me goodday, saying that he doubted if he should see me again.

When I came out of prison, — for some one interfered, and paid that tax, — I did not perceive that great changes had taken place on the common, such as he observed who went in a youth and emerged a tottering and gray-headed man; and yet a change had to my eyes come over the scene, — the town, and State, and country, — greater than any that mere time could effect. I saw yet more distinctly the State in which I lived. I saw to what extent the people among whom I lived could be trusted as good neighbors and friends; that their friendship was for summer weather only; that they did not greatly propose to do right; that they were a distinct race from me by their prejudices and superstitions, as the Chinamen and Malays are; that in their sacrifices to humanity they ran no risks, not even to their property; that after all they were not so noble but they treated the thief as he had treated them, and hope, by a certain outward observance and a few prayers, and by walking in a particular straight though useless path from time to time, to save their souls. This may be to judge my neighbors harshly; for I believe that many of them are not aware that they have such an institution as the jail in their village.

It was formerly the custom in our village, when a poor debtor came out of jail, for his acquaintances to salute him, looking through their fingers, which were crossed to represent the grating of a jail window, "How do ye do?" My neighbors did not thus salute me, but first looked at me, and then at one another, as if I had returned from a long journey. I was put into jail as I was going to the shoemaker's to get a shoe which was mended. When I was let out the next morning, I proceeded to finish my errand, and, having put on my mended shoe, joined a huckleberry party, who were impatient to put themselves under my conduct; and in half an hour, — for the horse was soon tackled, — was in the midst of a huckleberry field, on one of our highest hills, two miles off, and then the State was nowhere to be seen.

This is the whole history of "My Prisons."

I have never declined paying the highway tax, because I am as desirous of being a good neighbor as I am of being a bad subject; and as for supporting schools, I am doing my part to educate my fellow-countrymen now. It is for no particular item in the tax-bill that I refuse to pay it. I simply wish to refuse allegiance to the State, to withdraw and stand aloof from it effectually. I do not care to trace the course of my dollar, if I could, till it buys a man or a musket to shoot one with, — the dollar is innocent, — but I am concerned to trace the effects of my allegiance. In fact, I quietly declare war with the State, after my fashion, though I will still make what use and get what advantage of her I can, as is usual in such cases.

If others pay the tax which is demanded of me, from a sympathy with the State, they do but what they have already done in their own case, or rather they abet injustice to a greater extent than the State requires. If they pay the tax from a mistaken interest in the individual taxed, to save his property, or prevent his going to jail, it is because they have not considered wisely how far they let their private feelings interfere with the public good.

This, then, is my position at present. But one cannot be too much on his guard in such a case, lest his action be biased by obstinacy or an undue regard for the opinions of men. Let him see that he does only what belongs to himself and to the hour.

I think sometimes, Why, this people mean well, they are only ignorant; they would do better if they knew how: why give your neighbors this pain to treat you as they are not inclined to? But I think again, this is no reason why I should do as they do, or permit others to suffer much greater pain of a different kind. Again, I sometimes say to myself, When many millions of men, without heat, without ill will, without personal feeling of any kind, demand of you a few shillings only, without the possibility, such is their constitution, of retracting or altering their present demand, and without the possibility, on your side, of appeal to any other millions, why expose yourself to this overwhelming brute force? You do not resist cold and hunger, the winds and the waves, thus obstinately; you quietly submit to a thousand similar necessities. You do not put your head into the fire. But just in proportion as I regard this as not wholly a brute force, but partly a human force, and consider that I have relations to those millions as to so many millions of men, and not of mere brute or inanimate things, I see that appeal is possible, first and instantaneously, from them to the Maker of them, and, secondly, from them to themselves. But if I put my head deliberately into the fire, there is no appeal to fire or to the Maker of fire, and I have only myself to blame. If I could convince myself that I have any right to be satisfied with men as they are, and to treat them accordingly, and not according, in some respects, to my requisitions and expectations of what they and I ought to be, then, like a good Mussulman and fatalists, I should endeavor to be satisfied with things as they are, and say it is the will of God. And, above all, there is this difference between resisting this and a purely brute or natural force, that I can resist this with some effect; but I cannot expect, like Orpheus, to change the nature of the rocks and trees and beasts.

I do not wish to quarrel with any man or nation. I do not wish to split hairs, to make fine distinctions, or set myself up as better than my neighbors. I seek rather, I may say, even an excuse for conforming to the laws of the land. I am but too ready to conform to them. Indeed, I have reason to suspect myself on this head; and each year, as the tax-gatherer comes round, I find myself disposed to review the acts and position of the general and State governments, and the spirit of the people, to discover a pretext for conformity.

We must affect our country as our parents,
And if at any time we alienate
Our love or industry from doing it honor,
We must respect effects and teach the soul
Matter of conscience and religion,
And not desire of rule or benefit.

I believe that the State will soon be able to take all my work of this sort out of my hands, and then I shall be no better a patriot than my fellow-countrymen. Seen from a lower point of view, the Constitution, with all its faults, is very good; the law and the courts are very respectable; even this State and this American government are, in many respects, very admirable, and rare things, to be thankful for, such as a great many have described them; but seen from a point of view a little higher, they are what I have described them; seen from higher still, and the highest, who shall say what they are, or that they are worth looking at or thinking of at all?

However, the government does not concern me much, and I shall bestow the fewest possible thoughts on it. It is not many moments that I live under a government, even in this world. If a man is thought-free, fancy-free, imagination-free, that which is not never for a long time appearing to be to him, unwise rulers or reformers cannot fatally interrupt him.

I know that most men think differently from myself; but those whose lives are by profession devoted to the study of these or kindred subjects content me as little as any. Statesmen and legislators, standing so completely within the institution, never distinctly and nakedly behold it. They speak of moving society, but have no resting-place without it. They may be men of a certain experience and discrimination, and have no doubt invented ingenious and even useful systems, for which we sincerely thank them; but all their wit and usefulness lie within certain not very wide limits. They are wont to forget that the world is not governed by policy and expediency. Webster never goes behind government, and so cannot speak with authority about it. His words are wisdom to those legislators who contemplate no essential reform in the existing government; but for thinkers, and those who legislate for all time, he never once glances at the subject. I know of those whose serene and wise speculations on this theme would soon reveal the limits of his mind's range and hospitality. Yet, compared with the cheap professions of most reformers, and the still cheaper wisdom and eloquence of politicians in general, his are almost the only sensible and valuable words, and we thank Heaven for him. Comparatively, he is always strong, original, and, above all, practical. Still, his quality is not wisdom, but prudence. The lawyer's truth is not Truth, but consistency or a consistent expediency. Truth is always in harmony with herself, and is not concerned chiefly to reveal the justice that may consist with wrong-doing. He well deserves to be called, as he has been called, the Defender of the Constitution. There are really no blows to be given by him but defensive ones. He is not a leader, but a follower. His leaders are the men of '87. "I have never made an effort," he says, "and never propose to make an effort; I have never countenanced an effort, and never mean to countenance an effort, to disturb the arrangement as originally made, by which the various States came into the Union." Still thinking of the sanction which the Constitution gives to slavery, he says, "Because it was a part of the original compact, — let it stand." Notwithstanding his special acuteness and ability, he is unable to take a fact out of its merely political relations, and behold it as it lies absolutely to be disposed of by the intellect, — what, for instance, it behooves a man to do here in America to-day with regard to slavery, — but ventures, or is driven, to make some such desperate answer as the following, while professing to speak absolutely, and as a private man, — from which what new and singular code of social duties might be inferred? "The manner," says he, "in which the governments of those States where slavery exists are to regulate it is for their own consideration, under their responsibility to their constituents, to the general laws of propriety, humanity, and justice, and to God. Associations formed elsewhere, springing from a feeling of humanity, or any other cause, have nothing whatever to do with it. They have never received any encouragement from me, and they never will."

They who know of no purer sources of truth, who have traced up its stream no higher, stand, and wisely stand, by the Bible and the Constitution, and drink at it there with reverence and humility; but they who behold where it comes trickling into this lake or that pool, gird up their loins once more, and continue their pilgrimage toward its fountainhead.

No man with a genius for legislation has appeared in America. They are rare in the history of the world. There are orators, politicians, and eloquent men, by the thousand; but the speaker has not yet opened his mouth to speak who is capable of settling the much-vexed questions of the day. We love eloquence for its own sake, and not for any truth which it may utter, or any heroism it may inspire. Our legislators have not yet learned the comparative value of free-trade and of freedom, of union, and of rectitude, to a nation. They have no genius or talent for comparatively humble questions of taxation and finance, commerce and manufactures and agriculture. If we were left solely to the wordy wit of legislators in Congress for our guidance, uncorrected by the seasonable experience and the effectual complaints of the people, America would not long retain her rank among the nations. For eighteen hundred years, though perchance I have no right to say it, the New Testament has been written; yet where is the legislator who has wisdom and practical talent enough to avail himself of the light which it sheds on the science of legislation?

The authority of government, even such as I am willing to submit to, — for I will cheerfully obey those who know and can do better than I, and in many things even those who neither know nor can do so well, — is still an impure one: to be strictly just, it must have the sanction and consent of the governed. It can have no pure right over my person and property but what I concede to it. The progress from an absolute to a limited monarchy, from a limited monarchy to a democracy, is a progress toward a true respect for the individual. Even the Chinese philosopher was wise enough to regard the individual as the basis of the empire. Is a democracy, such as we know it, the last improvement possible in government? Is it not possible to take a step further towards recognizing and organizing the rights of man? There will never be a really free and enlightened State until the State comes to recognize the individual as a higher and independent power, from which all its own power and authority are derived, and treats him accordingly. I please myself with imagining a State at last which can afford to be just to all men, and to treat the individual with respect as a neighbor; which even would not think it inconsistent with its own repose if a few were to live aloof from it, not meddling with it, nor embraced by it, who fulfilled all the duties of neighbors and fellow-men. A State which bore this kind of fruit, and suffered it to drop off as fast as it ripened, would prepare the way for a still more perfect and glorious State, which also I have imagined, but not yet anywhere seen.

Ralph Henry Gabriel: EMERSON AND THOREAU

IN the middle period of the nineteenth century the village of Concord in the Commonwealth of Massachusetts stirred with new life. Here Hawthorne wrote polished studies of damaged souls; here Bronson Alcott turned from schoolmastering to philosophy. Here Emerson, during summer days, walked often along the town's main street past stores where farmers' families came to trade, and continued on the thoroughfare after it had become a dusty country road winding into the surrounding hills. At the northern edge of the village, the Concord River was crossed by a bridge where in 1775 the opening battle of the Revolution had been fought. The patriots of Concord proudly recalled that first blow struck for American liberty by Concord men. Their bridge was becoming a shrine to which pilgrims came to venerate the spot where Americans first died for the ideal of constitutional democracy. In 1837 Concord erected a battle monument beside the bridge. Concord, therefore, was no ordinary village metropolis of a rural area. It had a past. It was old — several times as old as contemporary villages of equal size in the Upper Mississippi Valley. Many of its houses were, according to American standards, venerable. The mood of Puritanism, which had dominated its thought in the seventeenth century, still clung to it like wisps of fog that the morning sun has not yet driven from the fields. In its periodic town meetings its quiet life was governed by the methods of a well-tried democracy. To these gatherings went Emerson, to discuss with his neighbors the problems of highway upkeep and the management of the Common.

Citizen Emerson was one of the atoms that made up the Concord community. So was his young friend, Henry Thoreau, who, by the 1850's, had acquired a reputation for being a little queer. There was mild neighborhood curiosity in 1845 concerning his lonely sojourn in a hut at Walden Pond not far away. In 1848 the villagers of Concord sometimes saw Thoreau working in Emerson's garden when the latter was in Europe. After the philosopher's return, the townspeople often watched the older and the younger man stride off together on a hike across the neighboring fields. There was some shaking of heads on the part of the church-goers. The proper business of a man, according to Puritan ethics, was work. To spend a week day alone or with a friend, as both Emerson and Thoreau frequently did, loitering about Walden Pond without even the excuse of hunting or fishing, was little short of a sin. To the scandal of the neighborhood, moreover, Thoreau refused to attend religious worship; Emerson, who had quit the ministry for what seemed to be no good cause, was only a little better. Emerson, however, was easily forgiven. He was a true son of Concord who, on the Fourth of

July, 1837, had disposed of the pretensions of the rival patriots of Lexington when he had read his "Concord Hymn" beside the new battle monument:

By the rude bridge that arched the flood,
  Their flag to April's breeze unfurled,
Here once the embattled farmers stood
  And fired the shot heard round the world.

Concord in the Middle Period was the scene of another battle. Like the tiff of April 19, 1775, this was also a fight for liberty. There were no shock troops engaged, however, for Emerson believed neither in numbers nor in disciples. He put his faith in battalions of one or two. Only such minorities, he thought, could accomplish concrete social advances. In Concord in the 1840's and 1850's, Emerson and Thoreau marched out, like the minute men of old, to fight for new ideals. The older man was not the originator of the democratic faith, for that cluster of social beliefs rose spontaneously among the Americans of his generation, but he was its greatest prophet. Emerson sensed the individualism of his rural America. He believed in it wholeheartedly, yet he felt that the emerging faith of democracy, in spite of its momentary victories, was imprisoned within a militant and advancing evangelical Christianity. Protestantism, he thought, was a lost cause. The problem of the hour for him was the rescue, from entangling Christian superstitions, of the great doctrines of the fundamental law, of progress, and of the free individual. When Harvard, his Alma Mater, refused to let him again speak to the student body after his address in 1838 to the Divinity School, he anticipated no quarter from his theological adversaries. As for Thoreau, he thought conventional Christianity little better than the medicine bundle carried by the Indian brave for protection.

In his later years Emerson, become famous, put shutters outside the lower half of his study windows to protect himself from the world. But in the two decades before the Civil War he traveled on lecture tours for thousands of miles in the crowded promiscuity of river steamboats and railroad trains. He knew the *genus Americanus* from first-hand contact. Emerson, like the commercial drummer, made his living by traveling, and the Concord philosopher was extraordinarily successful in vending his intellectual wares. His success creates a problem for the historian.

Emerson, who lectured quietly on the lyceum platform, was the antithesis of that familiar American type, the camp-meeting evangelist. No contrast could be more complete than that between the serenity of the scholar from Concord and the excited emotionalism of the exhorter. Nor was the difference limited to manner. Emerson's lectures were full of subtleties; their intellectual level was high; they usually contained passages which were over the heads of audiences untrained in philosophical thinking. By contrast, the preachers of evangelical Protestantism dispensed a simple theology. They did not normally tax the minds of their hearers; the clergy appealed from the head to the heart. The phenomenon of Emerson, ex-Unitarian minister from New England, making a success of lecturing in the trans-Appalachian stronghold of evangelical Protestantism in the middle decades of the nineteenth century is one of the more significant episodes of the age.

Emerson's success was not due to his preaching of a mystical, pantheistic transcendentalism. He talked to practical men for most of whom mysticism was, in all probability, incomprehensible. That particular type of religious experience has never been important in American culture. Emerson impressed the common folk of his generation because he preached a philosophy of individualism that not only seemed to set men free, but to provide them with dynamic, creative energy. He gave the doctrine of the free individual sharpness of definition, causing it to emerge, with the clarity of an etching, from the cloudy background of half-formulated ideas.

Throughout his early years Emerson struggled almost constantly with problems raised by the varieties of Christianity which were prevalent in the United States of his day. He never went through a Calvinist stage, so he did not have to formulate an answer to the problem of how to reconcile democracy's trust in the common man with Calvin's doctrine of the complete corruptness of human nature. Nor was Emerson compelled to undertake to harmonize Calvinistic determinism with the idea that in a democracy free men create and rule the government under which they live. For the early Emerson, Protestantism meant Unitarianism; one of the familiar stories in American history is the narrative of Emerson's growing discontent with the "pale negations" of this system, and his final decision to abandon the security of a comfortable pastorate for the hazards of independent lecturing and writing. Unitarianism, in Emerson's opinion, did not provide the dynamics which are necessary for individual creation. Unitarianism freed men from old superstitions but, when these had been thrown off, its power was spent.

Emerson, traveling over America, was aware of the forces released by evangelical Protestantism. He knew the power of that experience called conversion. He understood the evangelical concept of the free individual. But he had no use for the theology which lay behind the conversion, for it rested upon the authority of a literally inspired Scripture. For Emerson the Bible was no more inspired than some other great books. At best it recorded the experience with living of other men in other days. The poet-philosopher was willing to learn from the past, but he sought final sanctions in his own experience in the present. Man, thought Emerson, is a creature of nature. From nature he derives his individuality and his freedom. He must find in nature, rather than in the Bible, that ultimate authority which makes his freedom possible.

To Emerson the popular American version of the doctrine of the free individual was the beginning, rather than the end, of social philosophy. In American communities of the period, individualism meant the independence of the shopkeeper or of the husbandman, each man managing his affairs according to his lights and his tastes. Popular individualism emphasized social atoms; the one closely knit group which was universally recognized and approved was the family. To Emerson a man appeared to be part of something; Emerson's taste was for wholes rather than for parts. He rejected atomism, whether it appeared in social or in scientific thought. As an undergraduate at Harvard, he had studied natural philosophy only to find the scientists preoccupied with the parts of nature. Following the path of scientists since the days of Galileo and Newton, they broke down matter into molecules and molecules into atoms. But Emerson basically had as little sympathy for test tube seers as for crystal gazers. The philosophies of both were, in his opinion, destined to come to a bad end. The curse of science was its sole dependence upon the intellect. "Pure intellect," remarked Emerson, paying his respects to the eighteenth century Enlightenment, "is the pure devil when you have got off all the masks of Mephistopheles."[1] Reason, he observed, when men depend solely upon it, leads only to science. Feeling, to him, was as important as intellectual analyses in the apprehensions of nature, and, significant though science is, nature can teach man more than Newton's materialism. Scientific naturalism in Emerson's day emphasized the parts, the atoms which were thought to be the ultimate units of matter. It pictured the universe as a vast cosmic machine whose wheels within wheels fitted and worked together with infinite nicety. The incompleteness of the atom and of the individual man left Emerson dissatisfied; it outraged his aesthetic sense as did a musical discord. "To a sound judgment," he remarked, "the most abstract truth is the most practical."[2] He put behind him all systems which emphasized the many; he turned his thought — and his feelings — to the discovery of a philosophy of the one. By so doing he set his face against the prevailing winds of social and scientific thought in nineteenth century America. "Whoso would be a man must be a nonconformist,"[3] he explained quietly as he bested his way forward.

"We walked this afternoon to Edmund Hosmer's and Walden Pond," Emerson recorded in his journal on April 9, 1842. "The south wind blew and filled with bland and warm light the dry and sunny woods. The last year's leaves blew like birds through the air. As I sat on the bank of the Drop, or God's Pond, and saw the amplitude of the little water, what space, what verge, the little scudding fleets of ripples found to scatter and spread from side to side and take so

much time to cross the pond, and saw how the water seemed made for the wind and the wind for the water, dear playfellows for each other, — I said to my companion, I declare this world is so beautiful that I can hardly believe it exists."[4] Emerson did not see nature in one of its grander aspects as he walked that afternoon beside Walden Pond. Men stand in awe on the rim of the canyon of the Colorado or beneath El Capitan towering above the Merced. Emerson saw only a simple New England landscape, a commonplace composition which included water, a strip of sand and rocks, and the encircling woods. Any scientist could analyze it into its component parts. The farmers who tilled the fields lying on the flanks of the hills could do that and more. They knew where the muskrats built their tunnels and where, in the autumn, the farm dog was likely to tree a raccoon. The lore of the particular had no interest for Emerson that day at Walden. The aspect of the scene which impressed him was that "the water seemed made for the wind and the wind for the water." And the feeling came to him that he, an individual man, was made for both and both were made for him. The essence of the scene was the unity which bound the parts together and which fused the observer with the observed. In such fusion Emerson experienced the exaltation of a mystic. "The world is so beautiful," he said half in pain, "that I can hardly believe it exists." He made this unity his god. "We see the world by piece," he remarked at another time, "as the sun, the moon, the animal, the tree; but the whole, of which these are the shining parts, is the soul."[5] Emerson came to an understanding of

[1] Bliss Perry, *Heart of Emerson's Journals*, 207.
[2] R. W. Emerson, "Nature," *Emerson's Complete Works* (Riverside ed., 1883), I, 10.
[3] R. W. Emerson, "Self-Reliance," *Complete Works* (Riverside ed., 1883), II, 51.

[4] Perry, 152.
[5] R. W. Emerson, "Over-Soul," *Complete Works*, II, 253.

the nature and power of that vast impersonal spirit, that Over-Soul, which is the ultimate reality of nature. "Standing on the bare ground, — my head bathed in the blithe air, and uplifted into infinite space, — all mean egotism vanishes. I become a transparent eyeball; I am nothing; I see all; the currents of the Universal Being circulate through me; I am part or parcel of God."[6]

So Emerson penetrated, as he thought, the material husks of reality to its core. Looking out from here, as from the center of a sphere, the poet saw nature and man taking on new meanings. Nature "is a great shadow pointing always to the sun behind us." A man laboring for a brief day on the earth strives for food to eat and for protection against the elements. He has the body and some of the ways of an animal. He is a transient phenomenon important today, forgotten tomorrow. His petty, untutored egotism, like that of some self-important ant, causes him to listen wistfully to the preacher who asserts that man will live forever — in another world. What a picture, thought Emerson — the Christian preacher trying with a bellows of egotism to fan into flame that divine spark, the human soul. What is man? He is a conduit through which flows moral energy, the very essence of the Over-Soul. He is a part of God; his body is an instrument to work out the purposes of God. "Within man is the soul of the whole; the wise silence; the universal beauty, to which every part and particle is equally related; the eternal One."[7] And what of eternity? Emerson knew eternity that day at Walden Pond, when the breeze disturbed the leaves of other summers, for eternity is the realization of the unity between the transient individual and the everlasting One.

In this concept of the individual and of his relation to God may be found the key to Emerson's social philosophy. Society, he thought, is an aggregation of cohering individuals. The centrifugal forces tending to disrupt it are all too evident. They were clear enough in Emerson's day when section was muttering against section, and when the rich mill owner was too often ruthlessly exploiting the wage earner, his wife, and his child. The poor men of the East and of the West were asserting the power of their mass strength and, putting Andrew Jackson in the presidency, were smashing that symbol of financial autocracy, the great bank of the United States. Why did not democratic America, filled with greed and strife, collapse into futile chaos? Because within and behind all men was the eternal, stabilizing, unifying Over-Soul, God. The stresses in American society might seem alarming to little minds devoid of faith. They would not, however, prove fatal. Emerson welcomed even an increase of American heterogeneity. Let the immigrants come. "The energy of Irish, Germans, Swedes, Poles, and Cossacks, and all the European tribes, — and of the Africans, and of the Polynesians, — will construct a new race, a new religion, a new state, a new literature, which will be as vigorous as the new Europe which came out of the smelting-pot of the Dark Ages. . . ."[8] Here was a robust optimism born of faith.

Emerson had, however, few illusions concerning the breed of American politicians, local or national. He once remarked that, if he were ever in danger of loving life unduly, he would attend a

6 R. W. Emerson, "Nature," *op. cit.*, I, 15–16.

7 R. W. Emerson, "Over-Soul," *op. cit.*, II, 253.

8 Quoted by Stuart P. Sherman in *Essays and Poems of Emerson with an Introduction by Stuart P. Sherman*, 1921, xxxiv.

caucus of the followers of Andrew Jackson, and "I doubt not the unmixed malignity, the withering selfishness, the impudent vulgarity, that mark those meetings would speedily cure me of my appetite for longevity."[9] Yet his faith was invincible. Within each of these slattern democrats was the spirit of the One. The mechanic plying his trade or the farmer breaking the prairie held in his hand, if he could only be made to understand it, the hammer of Thor. One such Kansas husbandman, born of the common herd, sensed his power. He struck one blow for righteousness; America quaked from Cape Cod to the Rockies. Then John Brown of Osawatomie made "the gallows glorious like the cross."

To Emerson, Brown was merely another proof of the power and importance of the free individual. The philosopher himself was such a minority of one. He sought no disciples; he formed no cult. Emerson emphasized to enthusiastic admirers that no man could follow him step by step and be a disciple. All men are different; each expresses in his own peculiar way the Over-Soul within him. To attempt to superimpose upon dissimilar men an intellectual stereotype or a fixed pattern of action was for Emerson the unforgivable sin. Regimentation, he thought, destroyed the souls of men.

When Emerson was preparing the lectures published as *Essays, First Series,* the collectivist philosophy of Charles Fourier was much discussed in America. Albert Brisbane and Horace Greeley were its New-World prophets. The decade of the 1840's was a time of ferment as America slowly recovered from the depression of 1837–1842. American mores were not fixed; the desire for experiment was in the air. The famous Brook Farm Community near Concord did not at first

accept the Fourierist pattern, but tried out the collectivist ideas of the Concord transcendentalists. Emerson's attitude toward the Brook Farm venture illustrates the quality of his thought. He, the philosopher of individualism, did not dismiss collectivism with sarcasm. He attended the preliminary conferences which created the Farm. Here was a social experiment to be honestly undertaken. It might demonstrate that collectivism is the handmaid of individualism; it might prove that the soul of the individual man can develop more readily and express itself more freely in a communal than in a competitive social pattern. Emerson listened to the plans of the eager founders. On October 17, 1840, he set down his conclusions in his *Journal.* "Yesterday George and Sophia Ripley, Margaret Fuller and Alcott discussed here the Social Plans [Brook Farm]. I wished to be convinced, to be thawed, to be made nobly mad by the kindling before my eye of a new dawn of human piety. But this scheme was arithmetic and comfort; this was a hint borrowed from Tremont House and the United States Hotel; a rage in our poverty and politics to live rich and gentlemanlike, an anchor to leeward against a change of weather; a prudent forecast on the probable issue of the great questions of Pauperism and Poverty. And not once could I be inflamed, but sat aloof and thoughtless; my voice faltered and fell. It was not the cave of persecution which is the palace of spiritual power, but only a room in the Astor House hired for the Transcendentalists. I do not wish to remove from my present prison to a prison a little larger. I wish to break all prisons. I have not yet conquered my own house. It irks me and repents me. Shall I raise the siege of this hencoop, and march baffled away to a pretended

9 *Ibid.,* xxxii.

siege of Babylon? It seems to me that so to do were to dodge the problem I am set to solve, and to hide my impotency in the thick of a crowd. I can see too, afar, — that I should not find myself more than now, — no, not so much, in that select, but not by me selected, fraternity. Moreover, to join this body would be to traverse all my long-trumpeted theory, and the instinct which spoke from it, that one man is a counterpoise to a city, — that a man is stronger than a city, that his solitude is more prevalent and beneficent than the concert of crowds."[10]

So Emerson rejected the experimental collectivism of his day. It is the individual man in whose heart the Over-Soul, the Universal Mind, finds a dwelling place who is all important, Emerson concluded, in spite of Brook Farm. Standing on the frontier between the past, with its social heritage, and the future, with its promises, he fashions his own history and with it that of nations and of the world. Too long the dogmas of an outworn Christianity have kept man from understanding the power that lies within him. In the United States where the democratic faith provides the ideals by which to measure conduct, men are beginning to discover the individual, but their vision of what constitutes a man is blurred by old theologies. Teach these sons to know themselves and the nation will be on the march toward an empire of the spirit. Such an America, rising on the western shore of the Atlantic, must become a flaming beacon, lighting for all the world the path of human destiny.

"I spoke of friendship," wrote Emerson in his *Journal* in 1848, "but my friends and I are fishes in our habit. As for taking Thoreau's arm, I should as soon take the arm of an elm tree."[11] "Henry is military," he added five years later. "He seems stubborn and implacable; always manly and wise, but rarely sweet. One would say that, as Webster could never speak without an antagonist, so Henry does not feel himself except in opposition. He wants a fallacy to expose, a blunder to pillory, requires a little sense of victory, a roll of the drums, to call his powers into full exercise."[12] Emerson was, perhaps, a bit unfair to his young friend, who had been a member of his household, and who, after some schoolmastering and a little surveying, was in 1845 retiring from society to his hut on Walden Pond. *Walden,* which Thoreau distilled from that experiment, was more affirmation than rejection. Even so, to the end of his days the celibate pencil-maker remained an adversary of American civilization, a stiff-backed solitary soldier who tramped stubbornly in the opposite direction from the army's line of march.

Thoreau's New England was bustling with industrial enterprise. The Holyoke dam first successfully held back the Connecticut in 1849, the year in which Thoreau published *Civil Disobedience.* Almost every New England stream was turning the wheels of some mill or factory. Boston was the rendezvous of entrepreneurs great and small, men skilled in the stratagems and tactics, the deceptive retreats and surprise attacks essential to the art of pecuniary competition. Thoreau was shocked at the thought of a man spending his years at such an occupation when nature had given so short a time to live. In 1843 he read with growing anger in an English pamphlet of that economy of plenty which would result from the harnessing of the powers of

[10] Bliss Perry, *Heart of Emerson's Journals,* 156–157.

[11] *Ibid.,* 238.

[12] *Ibid.,* 263.

nature and making them serve men through machines. "Fellowmen!" exclaimed the enthusiastic innovator, J. A. Etzler, "I promise to show the means of creating a paradise within ten years, where everything desirable for human life may be had by every man in superabundance, without labor, and without pay."[13] For Thoreau machines were gadgets which made life so complicated that they made living difficult; they were burdens which men carried on their backs; they blighted alike the lives of the children who tended them in factories and of the entrepreneurs who had them built. Thoreau never compromised with the machine; he never ceased to despise — and to pity — those men whose days were filled with business and whose goal was wealth. Fortunes, like machines, increased the difficulty of living. Thoreau lived for many months in his hut at Walden to prove to himself and to whosoever might be interested that nature is sufficient, that the machine confines rather than frees the spirit. The machine, he thought, was becoming a menace to the free individual.

But a more serious danger, at the moment, was, in his opinion, the State. When he found the State dominated by the crude materialism of a rising industrialism, he withdrew and refused to pay his poll tax. His opposition to the body politic became embittered when the federal government called for soldiers for the war against Mexico in the years from 1846 to 1848. *Civil Disobedience,* written when Thoreau was thirty-two, is the best American expression of the philosophy that the State is potentially or actually a malevolent institution, a threat to the liberty of the individual, and, being such, an agency whose powers must be re-

13 Henry David Thoreau, *Writings of Thoreau* (New Riverside ed., 1893), X, 38.

duced to a minimum. Such an attitude had led to the writing of bills of rights into state constitutions during the Revolution and to the addition of the first ten amendments to the Constitution of 1787.

Thoreau's argument assumed that the individual comes into the world to live and not necessarily to make it better. This particular and separate personality has a conscience enabling him to know, and directing him to obey, the "higher law" of his nature. The citizen must not "resign his conscience to the legislator." He cannot accept the principle of majority rule; "any man more right than his neighbors constitutes a majority of one already." Majorities, in deciding what is expedient, rule by force. They make the law; the State is their instrument for its enforcement. "Laws never made a man a whit more just." The men who serve the government too often forget conscience and obey force; the State robs them of their manhood. "Visit the Navyyard," said Thoreau, "and behold a marine, such a man as an American government can make, or such as it can make a man with its black arts, — a mere shadow and reminiscence of humanity, a man laid out alive and standing, and already, as one may say, buried under arms." To Thoreau the professional soldier personified the negation of individual freedom.

If, perchance, the State be just, added the militant Thoreau, let the citizen share in its virtue. But if it be unjust, and such is the common characteristic of government, let him remember that "all men recognize the right of revolution; that is, the right to refuse allegiance to, and to resist the government, when its tyranny or its inefficiency are great and unendurable." Thoreau made no distinction between federal and local power; because Massachusetts did not refuse completely to co-operate in the war of spoliation against Mexico, he called her "a drab of state, a cloth-o'-silver slut." And it was a Massachusetts tax which he refused to pay. He advocated and practiced passive resistance.

Before his mind rose a vision of a better world, not the Paradise of the Christians, nor the communal utopia of the Fourierists, but one dominated by the individual, free in all things save in the right to violate his conscience. "There will never be a really free and enlightened State until the State comes to recognize the individual as a higher and independent power, from which all its own power and authority are derived, and treats him accordingly. I please myself with imagining a State at last which can afford to be just to all men, and to treat the individual with respect as a neighbor; which even would not think it inconsistent with its own repose if a few were to live aloof from it, not meddling with it, nor embraced by it, who fulfilled all the duties of neighbors and fellowmen. A State which bore this kind of fruit, and suffered it to drop off as fast as it ripened, would prepare the way for a still more perfect and glorious State, which also I have imagined, but not yet anywhere seen."[14] Disclaim it though he did, Thoreau was a crusader for a better world.

Thoreau was less interested in Protestantism than was Emerson, the ex-minister. The younger man dismissed Christianity as a spent force and, therefore a factor to be ignored. More than Emerson, Thoreau directed his thought toward the future. He saw, not always clearly, but with better vision than any of his contemporaries, new forces arising to threaten the great doctrines of the moral

law and of the free individual. One of these was industrialism, and another was nationalism which enhanced the power of the State. Had Thoreau not been stricken down in middle life, he would have lived to see the democratic faith bent to the service of the great industrialist and used to defend the economic overlord against majorities of weaker men seeking to put limits upon irresponsible and autocratic power. Thoreau, however, scented danger afar. He tried to establish, before it was too late, the conclusion that a philosophy of materialism is a formula of death. As for the second menace, the rising power of the State, Thoreau, happily, did not live to hear from across the ocean in the post-Versailles twentieth century the rhythm of the tramping feet of millions of men, of youths, and even of little children, or to see Christianity supplanted by State worship.

Emerson was often puzzled by the words and the doings of his brilliant friend. In spite of their mutual sympathy and of their common transcendentalism, they were, in some respects, far apart. The older man shook his head over the Walden experiment. "Henry Thoreau," he remarked, "is like the wood-god who solicits the wandering poet and draws him into antres vast and deserts idle, and bereaves him of his memory, and leaves him naked, plaiting vines and with twigs in his hand."[15] Thoreau's rebellion seemed to Emerson too much a matter of denials. So it was, for the naturalist was not given time to work his way through to the affirmations concerning the conduct of life which he wished one day to make, and which he hoped to find in a study of nature. Fate overruled him. One day in the spring of the year 1862, when McClellan in Virginia was preparing his

---

[14] See foregoing quotations from "Civil Disobedience," *Writings of Thoreau* (New Riverside ed., 1893), Vol. X.

[15] Perry, 238.

assault upon Richmond, Emerson wrote sadly in his *Journal*: "Sam Staples yesterday had been to see Henry Thoreau. 'Never spent an hour with more satisfaction. Never saw a man dying with so much pleasure and peace.'" On May 6 Thoreau passed, content with his denials and to leave the affirmations to other men.

Emerson and Thoreau lived in that epoch in which the American frontier was sweeping westward to the Pacific. On the edge of the wilderness, individualism was the normal and inevitable way of life. Here men, like Bill Williams, were free. Out of the frontier came American insistence upon personal liberty. But the freedom of Williams was that of escape. He abandoned a society whose growing complexity increased the problem of living. In the older communities, increase in numbers multiplied the restraints upon the individual man. The institutions which men established put them in shackles. The strong preyed upon the weak. For such problems the frontier, save only as it kept alive the ideal of the free individual, had no solution. It was a transient moment. And when it passed, the tasks of the East would become those of the West.

Emerson and Thoreau remained in New England in an environment in which, already, wealth was passing into the hands of the few. The rough equalitarianism of the frontier had long since disappeared. These two friends faced the issues of their day in the region where

solutions were hardest to find. Both were dissenters. Their significance lay in the fact that they served as spokesmen for an emerging democratic faith and, in so doing, gave comfort to men groping for enlightenment in an era in which society was closing in upon the individual. Emerson taught the individual the nobility of himself, the divinity of the average human. Thoreau insisted that the individual was right in his dissatisfaction with organized society, whether it was the college, the bank, the railroad, the Church, or the State. For both men the central problem was one of ethics, and the task of the moment was to make moral energy effective upon the earth. Both began with the doctrine of the fundamental law and interpreted it in ethical terms. Each insisted that human freedom is only achieved when men express, in their lives, that moral sentiment which permeates nature from the center of the cosmos to its circumference. Both were hopeful that the ideals of the democratic faith could be made to triumph over the materialism of American business and politics. Emerson expressed the mood of these two Concord rebels, who were carrying on the fight which had been started by the farmers at the bridge. "We are not minors and invalids," said the poet speaking for all Americans who venerated the idealism of democracy, "not cowards fleeing before a revolution, but guides, redeemers, benefactors, obeying the Almighty effort and advancing on Chaos and the Dark."[16]

16 R. W. Emerson, "Self-Reliance," *Complete Works*, II, 47.

Theodore Parker: TRANSCENDENTALISM

THE will is father to the deed, but the thought and sentiment are father and mother of the will. Nothing seems more impotent than a thought, it has neither hands nor feet, — but nothing proves so powerful. The thought turns out a thing; its vice or virtue becomes manners, habits, laws, institutions; the abstraction becomes concrete; the most universal proposition is the most particular; and in the end it is the abstract thinker who is the most practical man and sets mills a-running and ships to sail.

A change of ideas made all the difference between Catholic and Protestant, monarchical and democratic. You see that all things are first an idea in the mind, then a fact out of the mind. The architect, the farmer, the railroad-calculator, the founder of empires, has his temple, his farm, his railroad, or his empire, in his head as an idea before it is a fact in the world. As the thought is the thing becomes. Every idea bears fruit after its kind, — the good, good; the bad, bad. Some few hundred years ago John Huss, Luther, Lord Bacon, Descartes said, We will not be ruled by authority in the church or the school, but by common sense and reason. That was nothing but an idea; but out of it has come the Protestant Reformation, the English Revolution, the American Revolution, the French Revolution, the cycle of Revolutions that fill up the year 1848. Yes, all the learned societies of Europe, all the

Protestant churches, all the liberal governments, — of Holland, England, France, Germany, America, — have come of that idea. The old fellows in Galileo's time would not look through his telescope lest it should destroy the authorized theory of vision; they knew what they were about. So have all the old fellows known ever since who refuse to look through a new telescope, or even at it, but only talk against it. Once the Egyptian sculptors copied men into stone with their feet joined and their hands fixed to their sides. The copy indicated the immutableness of things in Egypt, where a mummy was the type of a man. A Greek sculptor separated the feet, as in life, illegally taking a live man for his type. The sculptor lost his head, for the government saw a revolution of the empire in this departure from the authorized type of man. Such is the power of ideas. The first question to ask of a civilized nation is, How do they think? what is their philosophy?

Now it is the design of philosophy to explain the phenomena of the universe by showing their order, connection, cause, law, use and meaning. These phenomena are of two kinds or forms, as they belong to the material world — facts of observation; and as they belong to the spiritual world — facts of consciousness: facts without, and facts within. From these two forms of phenomena or facts

Reprinted in *The World of Matter and the Spirit of Man* (Boston, American Unitarian Association, 1907).

there come two grand divisions of philosophy: the philosophy of outward things, — physics; the philosophy of inward things, — metaphysics.

In the material world, to us, there are only facts. Man carries something thither, to wit, ideas. Thus the world has quite a different look; for he finds the facts without have a certain relation to the ideas within. The world is one thing to Newton's dog Diamond, quite another to Newton himself. The dog saw only the facts and some of their uses; the philosopher saw therein the reflected image of his own ideas, — saw order, connection, cause, law and meaning, as well as use.

Now in the pursuit of philosophy there are two methods which may be followed, namely, the deductive and the inductive.

I. By the deductive the philosopher takes a certain maxim or principle, assumes it as a fact and therefrom deduces certain other maxims or principles as conclusions, as facts. But in the conclusions there must be nothing which is not in the primary fact else the conclusion does not conclude. All pure science is of this character — geometry, algebra, arithmetic. $1 + 1 = 2$ is a maxim, let us suppose: $1000 + 1000 = 2000$ is one deduction from it; $25 \times 25 = 625$, another deduction. Thus the philosopher must be certain of the fact he starts from, of the method he goes by, and the conclusion he stops at is made sure of beforehand.

The difficulty is that the philosopher often assumes his first fact, takes a fancy for a fact; then, though the method be right, the conclusion is wrong. For instance, Aristotle assumed this proposition, — the matter of the sun is incorruptible; thence he deduced this fact, that the sun does not change, that its light and heat are constant quantities. The conclusion did not agree with observation, the theory with the facts. His first fact was not proved, could not be,

was disproved. But when Galileo looked at the sun with a telescope he saw spots on the sun, movable spots. Aristotle's first fact turned out a fancy, so all conclusion from it. The Koran is written by the infallible inspiration of God, the Pope is infallible, the King can do no wrong, the People are always right, — these are assumptions. If taken as truths, you see the conclusions which may be deduced therefrom, — which have been. There is in God somewhat not wholly good, is an assumption which lies at the bottom of a good deal of theology, whence conclusions quite obvious are logically deduced, — 1, Manicheism, God and the devil; 2, God and an evil never to be overcome. God is absolute good is another assumption from which the opposite deductions are to be made. The method of deduction is of the greatest value and cannot be dispensed with.

II. By the inductive method the philosopher takes facts, puts them together after a certain order, seen in nature or devised in his own mind, and tries to find a more comprehensive fact common to many facts, i.e., what is called a *law*, which applies to many facts and so is a general law, or to all facts and so is a universal law. In the deductive method you pass from a universal fact to a particular fact; in the inductive, from the particular to the general. In the deductive process there is nothing in the conclusion which was not first in the premises; by the inductive something new is added at every step. The philosopher is sifting in his own conjecture or thought in order to get at a general idea which takes in all the particular facts in the case and explains them. When this general idea and the facts correspond the induction is correct. But it is as easy to arrive at a false conclusion by the inductive process as to assume a false maxim from which to make deductions. A physician's apprentice once visited his master's patient and found him dead, and reported the case accordingly. "What killed him?" said the old doctor. "He died of eating a horse." "Eating a horse!" expostulated the man of experience; "impossible! how do you know that?" "He did," said the inductive son of Æsculapius, "for I saw the saddle and bridle under the bed." Another, but a grown-up doctor, once gave a sick blacksmith a certain medicine; he recovered. *"Post hoc, ergo propter hoc,"* said the doctor, and tried the same drug on the next sick man, who was a shoemaker. The shoemaker died, and the doctor wrote down his induction: "This drug will cure all sick blacksmiths, but kill all sick shoemakers (Rule for phosphorus)."

The inductive method is also indispensable in all the sciences which depend on observation or experiment. The process of induction is as follows: After a number of facts is collected, the philosopher looks for some one fact common to all and explanatory thereof. To obtain this he assumes a fact as a law, and applies it to the facts before him. This is an hypothesis. If it correspond to the facts, the hypothesis is true. Two great forms of error are noticeable in the history of philosophy: 1, the assumption of false maxims, whence deductions are to be made, — the assumption of no-fact for a fact; 2, the making of false inductions from actual facts. In the first, a falsehood is assumed, and then falsehood deduced from it; in the second, from a truth falsehood is induced, and this new falsehood is taken as the basis whence other falsehoods are deduced.

Pythagoras declared the sun was the centre of the planets which revolved about it; that was an hypothesis, — guesswork, and no more. He could not compare the hypothesis with facts, so his hypothesis could not be proved or disproved. But long afterwards others made the comparison and confirmed the hypothesis. Kepler wished to find out what ratio the time of a planet's revolution bears to its distance from the sun. He formed an hypothesis, — "The time is proportionable to the distance." No, that did not agree with the facts. "To the square of the distance?" No. "To the cube of the distance?" No. "The square of the time to the cube of the distance?" This he found to be the case, and so he established his celebrated law, — Kepler's third law. But he examined only a few planets: how should he know the law was *universal?* He could not learn that by induction. That would only follow from this postulate, "The action of nature is always uniform," which is not an induction, nor a deduction, but an assumption. The inductive method alone never establishes a universal law, for it cannot transcend the particular facts in the hands of the philosopher. The axioms of mathematics are not learned by inductions, but assumed outright as self-evident. "Kepler's third law is universal of all bodies moving about a centre," — now there are three processes by which that conclusion is arrived at: 1. The process of induction, by which the law is proved general and to apply to all the cases investigated. 2. A process of deduction from the doctrine or axiom, that the action of nature is always uniform. 3. That maxim is obtained by a previous process of assumption from some source or another.

Such is the problem of philosophy, to explain the facts of the universe; such the two departments of philosophy, physics and metaphysics; such the two methods of inquiry, deductive and inductive; such are the two forms of error, — the assumption of a false fact as the starting-point of deduction, the induction of a false fact by the inductive process. Now these methods are of use in each department of philosophy, indispensable in each, in physics and in metaphysics.

This is the problem of metaphysics, — to explain the facts of human consciousness. In metaphysics there are and have long been two schools of philosophers. The first is the sensational school. Its most important metaphysical doctrine is this: There is nothing in the intellect which was not first in the senses. Here "intellect" means the whole intellectual, moral, affectional and religious consciousness of man. The philosophers of this school claim to have reached this conclusion legitimately by the inductive method. It was at first an hypothesis; but after analyzing the facts of consciousness, interrogating all the ideas and sentiments and sensations of man, they say the hypothesis is proved by the most careful induction. They appeal to it as a principle, as a maxim, from which other things are deduced. They say that experience by one or more of the senses is the ultimate appeal in philosophy: all that I know is of sensational origin; the senses are the windows which let in all the light I have; the senses afford a sensation. I reflect upon this, and by reflection transform a sensation into an idea. An idea, therefore, is a transformed sensation.

A school in metaphysics soon becomes a school in physics, in politics, ethics, religion. The sensational school has been long enough in existence to assert itself in each of the four great forms of human action. Let us see what it amounts to.

I. In physics. 1. It does not afford us a certainty of the existence of the outward world. The sensationalist believes it, not on account of his sensational philosophy, but in spite of it; not by his philosophy, but by his common sense:

he does not philosophically know it. While I am awake the senses give me various sensations, and I refer the sensations to an object out of me, and so perceive its existence. But while I am asleep the senses give me various sensations, and for the time I refer the sensations to an object out of me, and so perceive its existence, — but when I awake it seems a dream. Now, if the senses deceive me in sleep, why not when awake? How can I *know* philosophically the existence of the material world? With only the sensational philosophy I cannot! I can only *know* the facts of consciousness. I cannot pass from ideas to things, from psychology to ontology. Indeed there is no ontology, and I am certain only of my own consciousness. Bishop Berkeley, a thorough sensationalist, comes up with the inductive method in his hand, and annihilates the outward material world, annihilates mankind, leaves me nothing but my own consciousness, and no consciousness of any certainty there. Dr. Priestley, a thorough sensationalist, comes up with the same inductive method in his hand, and annihilates the spiritual world, annihilates the soul. Berkeley, with illogical charity, left me the soul as an existence, but stripped me of matter; I was certain I had a soul, not at all sure of my body. Priestley, as illogically, left me the body as an existence, but stripped me of the soul. Both of these gentlemen I see were entirely in the right, if their general maxim be granted; and so, between the two, I am left pretty much without soul or sense! Soul and body are philosophically hurled out of existence!

From its hypothetical world sensationalism proceeds to the laws of matter; but it cannot logically get beyond its facts. Newton says, "Gravitation prevails, — its power diminishing as the square of the distance increases between two bodies, so far as I have seen." "Is it so where you have not seen?" Newton doesn't know; he cannot pass from a general law to a universal law. As the existence of the world is hypothetical, so the universality of laws of the world is only hypothetical universality. The Jesuits who edited the Principia were wise men when they published them as an hypothesis.

The sensational philosophy has prevailed chiefly in England; that is the home of its ablest representatives, — Bacon, Locke. See the effect. England turns her attention to sciences that depend chiefly on observation, on experiment, — botany, chemistry, the descriptive part of astronomy, zoology, geology. England makes observations on the tides, on variations of the magnetic needle, on the stars; fits out exploring expeditions; learns the facts; looks after the sources of the Nile, the Niger; hunts up the North Pole; tests the strength of iron, wood, gunpowder; makes improvements in all the arts, in mechanics. But in metaphysics she does nothing; in the higher departments of physics — making comprehensive generalizations — she does little. Even in mathematics, after Newton, for a hundred years England fell behind the rest of Europe. She is great at experiment, little at pure thinking.

The sensational philosophy has no idea of cause, except that of empirical connection in time and place; no idea of substance, only of body, or form of substance; no ontology, but phenomenology. It refers all questions — say of the planets about the sun — to an outward force: when they were made, God, standing outside, gave them a push and set them a-going; or else their motion is the result of a fortuitous concourse of atoms, a blind fate. Neither conclusion is a philosophical conclusion, each an hypothesis.

Its physics are mere materialism; hence it delights in the atomistic theory of nature and repels the dynamic theory of matter. The sensationalist's physics appear well in a celebrated book, "The Vestiges of the Natural History of Creation." The book has many valuable things in it, but the philosophy of its physics is an unavoidable result of sensationalism. There is nothing but materialism in his world. All is material, effects material, causes material, his God material, — not surpassing the physical universe, but co-extensive therewith. In zoology life is the result of organization, but is an immanent life. In anthropology the mind is the result of organization, but is an immanent mind; in theology God is the result of organization, but is an immanent God. Life does not *transcend* organization, nor does mind, nor God. All is matter.

II. In politics. Sensationalism knows nothing of absolute right, absolute justice; only of historical right, historical justice. "There is nothing in the intellect which was not first in the senses." The senses by which we learn of justice and right are hearing and seeing. Do I reflect, and so get a righter right and juster justice than I have seen or heard of, it does me no good, for "nothing is in the intellect which was not in the senses." Thus absolute justice is only a whim, a no-thing, a dream. Men that talk of absolute justice, absolute right, are visionary men.

In politics, sensationalism knows nothing of ideas, only of facts; "the only lamp by which its feet are guided is the lamp of experience." All its facts are truths of observation, not of necessity. "There is no right but might," is the political philosophy of sensationalism. It may be the might of a king, of an aristocracy, of a democracy, the might of passions, the might of intellect, the might of muscle, — it has a right to what it will. It appeals always to human history, not human nature. Now human history shows what has been, not what should be or will be. To reason about war it looks not to the natural justice, only to the cost and present consequences. To reason about free trade or protection, it looks not to the natural justice or right of mankind, but only to the present expediency of the thing. Political expediency is the only right or justice it knows in its politics. So it always looks back, and says "it worked well at Barcelona or Venice," or "did not work well." It loves to cite precedents out of history, not laws out of nature. It claims a thing not as a human right, but as an historical privilege received by Magna Charta or the Constitution; as if a right were more of a right because time-honored and written on parchment; or less, because just claimed and for the first time and by a single man. The sensationalist has no confidence in ideas, so asks for facts to hold on to and to guide him in his blindness. Said a governor in America, "The right of suffrage is universal." "How can that be," said a sensationalist, "when the Constitution of the state declares that certain persons shall not vote?" He knew no rights before they became constitutional, no rights but vested rights, — perhaps none but "invested."

The sensationalists in politics divide into two parties, each with the doctrine that in politics "might makes right." One party favors the despotism of the few, — is an oligarchy; or of the one, — is a monarchy. Hence the doctrine is, "The king can do no wrong." All power is his; he may delegate it to the people as a privilege; it is not theirs by right, by nature, and his as a trust. He has a right to make any laws he will, not merely any just laws. The people must pay passive obedience to the king, he has eminent domain over them. The celebrated Thomas Hobbes is the best representative of this party, and has one great merit, — of telling what he thought.

The other party favors the despotism of the many, — is a democracy. The doctrine is, "The people can do no wrong." The majority of the people have the right to make any laws they will, not merely any just laws; and the minority must obey, right or wrong. You must not censure the measures of the majority, you afford "aid and comfort to the enemy." The state has absolute domain over the citizen, the majority over the minority; this holds good of the voters, and of any political party in the nation. For the majority has power of its own right, for its own behoof; not in trust, and for the good of all and each! The aim of sensational politics is the greatest good of the greatest number; this may be obtained by sacrificing the greatest good of the lesser number, — by sacrificing any individual, — or sacrificing absolute good. In No-man's-land this party prevails: the dark-haired men, over forty million, — the red-haired, only three million five hundred thousand, — the dark-haired enslave the red-haired, for the greatest good of the greatest number. But in a hundred years the red-haired men are most numerous, and turn round and enslave the black-haired.

Thomas Paine is a good representative of this party; so is Marat, Robespierre, the author of the "Système de la Nature." In the old French Revolution you see the legitimate consequence of this doctrine, that might makes right, that there is no absolute justice, in the violence, the murder, the wholesale assassination. The nation did to masses, and in the name of democracy, what all kings had done to the nation and in the name of monarchy, — sought the greatest good of the controlling power at the sacrifice of an opponent. It is the same maxim which in cold blood hangs a single culprit, enslaves three million negroes, and butchers thousands of men as in the September massacres. The sensational philosophy established the theory that might makes right, — and the mad passions of a solitary despot, or a million-headed mob, made it a fact. Commonly the two parties unite by a compromise, and then it consults not the greatest good of its king alone, as in a brutal, pure monarchy; not of the greatest number, as in a pure and brutal democracy; but the greatest good of a class, — the nobility and gentry in England, the landed proprietors and rich burghers in Switzerland, the slaveholders in South Carolina. Voltaire is a good representative of this type of sensational politics, not to come nearer home. In peaceful times England shares the defect of the sensational school in politics. Her legislation is empirical; great ideas do not run through her laws; she loves a precedent better than a principle; appeals to an accidental fact of human history, not an essential fact of human nature which is prophetic. Hence legislative politics is not a great science which puts the facts of human consciousness into a state, making natural justice common law; nothing but a poor dealing with precedents, a sort of national housekeeping and not very thrifty housekeeping. In our own nation you see another example of the same, — result of the same sensational philosophy. There is no right, says Mr. Calhoun, but might; the white man has that, so the black man is his political prey. And Mr. Polk tells us that Vermont, under the Constitution, has the same right to establish slavery as Georgia to abolish it.

III. In ethics. Ethics are the morals of the individual; politics of the mass. The sensationalist knows no first truths in morals; the source of maxims in morals is experience; in experience there is no absolute right. Absolute justice, absolute right, were never in the senses, so not in the intellect; only whimsies, words in the mouth. The will is not free, but wholly conditioned, in bondage; character made always for you, not by you. The intellect is a smooth table; the moral power a smooth table; and experience writes there what she will, and what she writes is law of morality. Morality is expediency, nothing more; nothing is good of itself, right of itself, just of itself, — but only because it produces agreeable consequences, which are agreeable sensations. Dr. Paley is a good example of the sensational moralist. I ask him "What is right, just?" He says, "There are no such things; they are the names to stand for what works well in the long run." "How shall I know what to do in a matter of morals? by referring to a moral sense?" "Not at all: only by common sense, by observation, by experience, by learning what works well in the long run; by human history, not human nature. To make a complete code of morals by sensationalism you must take the history of mankind, and find what has worked well, and follow that because it worked well." "But human history only tells what has been and worked well, not what is right. I want what is right!" He answers, "It is pretty much the same thing." "But suppose the first men endowed with faculties perfectly developed, would they know what to do?" "Not at all. Instinct would tell the beast antecedent to experience, but man has no moral instinct, must learn only by actual trial." "Well," say I, "let alone that matter, let us come to details. What is honesty?" "It is the best policy." "Why must I tell the truth, keep my word, be chaste, temperate?" "For the sake of the reward, the respect of your fellows, the happiness of a long life and heaven at last. On the whole God pays well for virtue; though slow pay, he is sure." "But suppose the devil paid the better pay?" "Then serve him, for the end is not the service, but the pay. Virtue, and by virtue I mean all moral excellence, is not a good in itself, but good as producing some other good." "Why should I be virtuous?" "For the sake of the reward." "But vice has its rewards, they are present and not future, immediate and certain, not merely contingent and mediate. I should think them greater than the reward of virtue." Then vice to you is virtue, for it pays best. The sensational philosophy knows no conscience to sound in the man's ears the stern word, Thou oughtest so to do, come what will come!

In politics might makes right, so in morals. Success is the touchstone; the might of obtaining the reward the right of doing the deed. Bentham represents the sensational morals of politics; Paley of ethics. Both are Epicureans. The sensationalist and the Epicurean agree in this, — enjoyment is the touchstone of virtue and determines what is good, what bad, what indifferent: this is the generic agreement. Heathen Epicurus spoke only of enjoyment in this life; Christian Archdeacon Paley — and a very *arch*deacon — spoke of enjoyment also in the next: this is the specific difference. In either case virtue ceases to be virtue, for it is only a bargain.

There is a school of sensationalists who turn off and say, "Oh, you cannot answer the moral questions and tell what is right, just, fair, good. We must settle that by revelation." That, of course, only adjourns the question and puts the decision on men who received the revelation or God who made it. They do not meet the philosopher's question; they assume that the difference between right and wrong is not knowable by human faculties, and, if there be any difference between right and wrong, there is no faculty in man which naturally loves right and abhors wrong, still less any faculty which can find out what *is* right, what wrong. So all moral questions are to be decided by authority, because somebody said so; not by reference to facts of consciousness, but to phenomena of history. Of course the moral law is not a law which is of me, rules in me and by me; only one put on me, which rules over me! Can any lofty virtue grow out of this theory? any heroism? Verily not. Regulus did not ask a reward for his virtue; if so, he made but a bargain, and who would honor him more than a desperate trader who made a good speculation? There is something in man which scoffs at expediency; which will do right, justice, truth, though hell itself should gape and bid him hold his peace; the morality which anticipates history, loves the right for itself. Of this Epicurus knew nothing, Paley nothing, Bentham nothing, sensationalism nothing. Sensationalism takes its standard of political virtue from the House of Commons; of right from the Constitution and common law; of commercial virtue from the board of brokers at their best, and the old bankrupt law; or virtue in general from the most comfortable classes of society, from human history, not human nature; and knows nothing more. The virtue of a Regulus, of a Socrates, of a Christ, it knows not.

See the practical effect of this. "A young man goes into trade. Experience meets him with the sensationalist morals in its hand, and says, " '*Caveat emptor*, Let the buyer look to it, not you'; you must be righteous, young man, but not righteous overmuch; you must tell the truth to all who have the right to ask you, and when and where they have a right to ask you, — otherwise you may lie. The mistake is not in lying, or deceit; but in lying and deceiving to your own disadvantage. You must not set up a private conscience of your own in your trade, you will lose the confidence of respectable people. You must have a code of morals which works well and produces agreeable sensations in the long run. To learn the true morals of business you must not ask conscience, that is a whim and very unphilosophical. You must ask, How did Mr. Smith make his money? He cheated, and so did Mr. Brown and Mr. Jones, and they cheat all round. Then you must do the same, only be careful not to cheat so as to 'hurt your usefulness' and 'injure your reputation.'"

Shall I show the practical effects of this, not on very young men, in politics? It would hurt men's feelings, and I have no time for that.

IV. In religion. Sensationalism must have a philosophy of religion, a theology; let us see what theology. There are two parties; one goes by philosophy, the other mistrusts philosophy.

1. The first thing in theology is to know God. The idea of God is the touchstone of a theologian. Now to know the existence of God is to be certain thereof as of my own existence. "Nothing in the intellect which was not first in the senses," says sensationalism; "all comes by sensational experience and reflection thereon." Sensationalism — does that give us the idea of God? I ask the sensationalist, "Does the sensational eye see God?" "No." "The ear hear him?" "No." "Do the organs of sense touch or taste him?" "No." "How then do you get the idea of God?" "By induction from facts of ob-

servation *a posteriori*. The senses deal with finite things; I reflect on them, put them all together I assume that they have *cause;* then by the inductive method I find out the character of that cause: that is God." Then I say, "But the senses deal with only finite things, so you must infer only a finite maker, else the induction is imperfect. So you have but a finite God. Then these finite things, measured only by my experience, are imperfect things. Look at disorders in the frame of nature; the sufferings of animals, the miseries of men; here are seeming imperfections which the sensational philosopher staggers at. But to go on with this induction: from an imperfect work you must infer an imperfect author. So the God of sensationalism is not only finite, but imperfect even at that. But am I certain of the existence of the finite and imperfect God? The existence of the outward world is only an hypothesis, its laws hypothetical; all that depends on that or them is but an hypothesis, — the truth of your faculties, the forms of matter only on hypothesis: so the existence of God is not a certainty; he is but our hypothetical God. But a hypothetical God is no God at all, not the living God: an imperfect God is no God at all, not the true God: a finite God is no God at all, not the absolute God. But this hypothetical, finite, imperfect God, where is he? In matter? No. In spirit? No. Does he act in matter or spirit? No, only now and then he did act by miracle; he is outside of the world of matter and spirit. Then he is a nonresident, an absentee. A non-resident God is no God at all, not the all-present God."

The above is the theory on which Mr. Hume constructs his notion of God with the sensational philosophy, the inductive method; and he arrives at the hypothesis of a God, of a finite God, of an imperfect God, of a non-resident God. Beyond that the sensational philosophy as philosophy cannot go.

But another party comes out of the same school to treat of religious matters; they give their philosophy a vacation, and to prove the existence of God they go back to tradition, and say, "Once God revealed himself to the senses of men; they heard him, they saw him, they felt him; so to them the existence of God was not an induction, but a fact of observation; they told it to others, through whom it comes to us; we can say it is not a fact of observation but a fact of testimony."

"Well," I ask, "are you certain then?" "Yes." "Quite sure? Let me look. The man to whom God revealed himself may have been mistaken; it may have been a dream, or a whim of his own, perhaps a fib; at any rate, he was not philosophically certain of the existence of the outward world in general; how could he be of anything that took place in it? Next, the evidence which relates the transaction is not wholly reliable: how do I know the books which tell of it tell the truth, that they were not fabricated to deceive me? All that rests on testimony is a little uncertain if it took place one or two thousand years ago; especially if I know nothing about the persons who testify or of that whereof they testify; still more so if it be a thing, as you say, unphilosophical and even supernatural."

So, then, the men who give a vacation to their philosophy have slurred the philosophical argument for a historical, the theological for the mythological, and have gained nothing except the tradition of God. By this process we are as far from the infinite God as before, and have only arrived at the same point where the philosophy left us.

The English Deists and the Socinians and others have approached religion with the sensational philosophy in their hands; we are to learn of God philosophically only by induction. And such is their God. They tell us that God is not knowable; the existence of God is not a certainty to us; it is a probability, a credibility, a possibility, — a certainty to none. You ask of sensationalism, the greatest question, "Is there a God?" Answer: "Probably." "What is his character?" "Finite, imperfect." "Can I trust him?" "If we consult tradition it is creditable; if philosophy, possible."

2. The next great question in theology is that of the immortality of the soul. That is a universal hope of mankind; what does it rest on? Can I know my immortality? Here are two wings of the sensational school. The first says, "No, you cannot know it; it is not true. Mind, soul, are two words to designate the result of organization. Man is not a mind, not a soul, not a free will. Man is a body, with blood, brains, nerves — nothing more; the organization gone, all is gone." Now that is sound, logical, consistent; that was the conclusion of Hume, of many of the English Deists, and of many French philosophers in the last century; they looked the fact in the face. But mortality, annihilation, is rather an ugly fact to look fairly in the face; but Mr. Hume and others have done it, and died brave with the sensational philosophy.

The other wing of the sensational school gives its philosophy another vacation, rests the matter not on philosophy but history; not on the theological but the mythological argument; on authority of tradition asserting a phenomenon of human history, they try to establish the immortality of man by a single precedent, a universal law by the tradition of a single, empirical, contingent phenomenon.

But I ask the sensational philosopher, "Is immortality certain?" "No." "Probable?" "No." "Credible?" "No." "Possible?" "Barely." I ask the traditional division, "Is immortality certain?" "No, it is left uncertain to try your faith." "Is it probable?" "Yes, there is one witness in six thousand years, one out of ten million times ten million." "Well, suppose it is probable; is immortality, if it be, sure to be a good thing, for me, for mankind?" "Not at all! There is nothing in the nature of man, nothing in the nature of the world, nothing in the nature of God to make you sure immortality will prove a blessing to mankind in general, to yourself in special!"

3. That is not quite all. Sensationalism does not allow freedom of the will; I say not, absolute freedom — that belongs only to God, — but it allows no freedom of the will. See the result: all will is God's, all willing therefore is equally divine, and the worst vice of Pantheism follows. "But what is the will of God, is that free?" "Not at all; man is limited by the organization of his body, God by the organization of the universe." So God is not absolute God, not absolutely free; and as man's will is necessitated by God's, so God's will by the universe of matter; and only a boundless fate and pitiless encircles man and God.

This is the philosophy of sensationalism; such its doctrine in physics, politics, ethics, religion. It leads to boundless uncertainty. Berkeley resolves the universe into subjective ideas; no sensationalist knows a law in physics to be universal. Hobbes and Bentham and Condillac in politics know of no right but might; Priestley denies the spirituality of man, Collins and Edwards his liberty; Dodwell

affirms the materiality of the soul, and the mortality of all men not baptized; Mandeville directly, and others indirectly, deny all natural distinction between virtue and vice; Archdeacon Paley knows no motive but expediency.

The materialist is puzzled with the existence of matter; finds its laws general, not universal. The sensational philosophy meets the politician and tells him through Rousseau and others, "Society has no divine original, only the social compact; there is no natural justice, natural right; no right, but might; no greater good than the greatest good of the greatest number, and for that you may sacrifice all you will; to defend a constitution is better than to defend justice." In morals the sensational philosophy meets the young man and tells him all is uncertain; he had better be content with things as they are, himself as he is; to protest against a popular wrong is foolish, to make money by it, or ease, or power, is a part of wisdom; only the fool is wise above what is written. It meets the young minister with its proposition that the existence of God is not a certainty, nor the immortality of the soul; that religion is only traditions of the elders and the keeping of a form. It says to him, "Look there, Dr. Humdrum has got the tallest pulpit and the quietest pews, the fattest living and the cosiest nook in all the land; how do you think he won it? Why, by letting well enough alone; he never meddles with sin; it would break his heart to hurt a sinner's feelings, — he might lose a parishioner; he never dreams to make the world better, or better off. Go thou and do likewise."

I come now to the other school. This is distinguished by its chief metaphysical doctrine, that there is in the intellect (or consciousness), something that never was in the senses, to wit, the intellect (or consciousness) itself; that man has faculties which transcend the senses; faculties which give him ideas and intuitions that transcend sensational experience; ideas whose origin is not from sensation, nor their proof from sensation. This is the transcendental school. They maintain that the mind (meaning thereby all which is not sense) is not a smooth tablet on which sensation writes its experience, but is a living principle which of itself originates ideas when the senses present the occasion; that, as there is a body with certain senses, so there is a soul or mind with certain powers which give the man sentiments and ideas. This school maintains that it is a fact of consciousness itself that there is in the intellect somewhat that was not first in the senses; and also that they have analyzed consciousness, and by the inductive method established the conclusion that there is a consciousness that never was sensation, never could be; that our knowledge is in part *a priori;* that we know, 1, certain truths of necessity; 2, certain truths of intuition, or spontaneous consciousness; 3, certain truths of demonstration, a voluntary consciousness; all of these truths, not dependent on sensation for cause, origin, or proof. Facts of observation, sensational experience, it has in common with the other school.

Transcendentalism, also, reports itself in the four great departments of human activity — in physics, politics, ethics, religion.

I. In physics it starts with the maxim that the senses acquaint us actually with body, and therefrom the mind gives us the idea of substance, answering to an objective reality. Thus is the certainty of the material world made sure of. Then *a priori* it admits the uniformity of the action of nature; and its laws are *a priori* known to be universal, and not general alone. These two doctrines it finds as maxims resulting from the nature of man, facts given. Then it sets out with other maxims, first truths, which are facts of necessity, known to be such without experience. All the first truths of mathematics are of this character, *e.g.,* that the whole is greater than a part. From these, by the deductive method, it comes at other facts, — facts of demonstration; these also are transcendental, that is, transcend the senses, transcend the facts of observation. For example, the three angles of a triangle are equal to two right angles, — that is universally true; it is a fact of demonstration, and is a deduction from a first truth which is self-evident, a fact of necessity. But here the fact of demonstration transcends the fact of experience, philosophy is truer than sensation. The whole matter of geometry is transcendental.

Transcendentalism does not take a few facts out of human history and say they are above nature; all that appears in nature it looks on as natural, not supernatural, not subternatural; so the distinction between natural and supernatural does not appear. By this means philosophy is often in advance of observation; *e.g.,* Newton's law of gravitation, Kepler's third law, the theory that a diamond might be burned, and Berkeley's theory of vision, — these are interpretations of nature, but also anticipations of nature, as all true philosophy must be. Those men, however, did not philosophically know it to be so. So by an actual law of nature, not only are known facts explained, but the unknown anticipated.

Evils have come from the transcendental method in physics; men have scorned observation, have taken but a few facts from which to learn universal laws, and so failed of getting what is universal, even general. They have tried to divine the constitution of the world, to do without sensational experience in matters where knowledge depends on that and that is the *sine quâ non*. The generalizations of the transcendental naturalists have been often hasty; they attempt to determine what nature shall be, not to learn what nature is. Thus a famous philosopher said there are only seven primary planets in the solar system, and from the nature of things, *a priori* known, it is impossible there should be more. He had intelligence in advance of the mail; but the mail did not confirm, for six months afterwards Dr. Piazzi discovered one of the asteroids; and in a few years three more were found, and now several more have been discovered, not to mention the new planet Neptune. Many of the statements of Schelling in physics are of this same character.

II. In politics, transcendentalism starts not from experience alone, but from consciousness; not merely from human history, but also from human nature. It does not so much quote precedents, contingent facts of experience, as ideas, necessary facts of consciousness. It only quotes the precedent to obtain or illustrate the idea. It appeals to a natural justice, natural right; absolute justice, absolute right. Now the source and original of this justice and right it finds in God — the conscience of God; the channel through which we receive this justice and right is our own moral sense, our conscience, which is our consciousness of the conscience of God. This conscience in politics and in ethics transcends experience, and *a priori* tells us of the just, the right, the good, the fair; not the relatively right alone, but absolute right also. As it transcends experience, so it anticipates history; and the ideal justice of conscience is juster than the empirical and contingent justice actually exercised at Washington or at Athens, as the ideal circle is rounder than one the stone-cutter scratches on his rough seal. In transcendental politics the question of expediency is always subordinate to the question of natural right; it asks not merely about the cost of a war, but its natural justice. It aims to organize the ideals of man's moral and social nature into political institutions; to have a government which shall completely represent the facts of man's social consciousness so far as his nature is now developed. But as this development is progressive, so must government be; yet not progressive by revolution, by violence; but by harmonious development, progressive by growth. The transcendental politician does not merely interpret history, and look back to Magna Charta and the Constitution; but into human nature, through to divine nature; and so anticipates history, and in man and God finds the origin and primary source of all just policy, all right legislation. So looking he transcends history.

For example, the great political idea of America, the idea of the Declaration of Independence, is a composite idea made up of three simple ones: 1. Each man is endowed with certain unalienable rights. 2. In respect of these rights all men are equal. 3. A government is to protect each man in the entire and actual enjoyment of all the unalienable rights. Now the first two ideas represent ontological facts, facts of human consciousness; they are facts of necessity. The third is an idea derived from the two others, is a synthetic judgment *a priori*; it was not learned from sensational experience; there never was a government which did this, nor is there now. Each of the other ideas transcended history:

every unalienable right has been alienated, still is; no two men have been actually equal in actual rights. Yet the idea is true, capable of proof by human nature, not of verification by experience; as true as the proposition that three angles of a triangle are equal to two right angles; but no more capable of a sensational proof than that. The American Revolution, with American history since, is an attempt to prove by experience this transcendental proposition, to organize the transcendental idea of politics. The idea demands for its organization a democracy — a government of all, for all, and by all; a government by natural justice, by legislation that is divine as much as a true astronomy is divine, legislation which enacts law representing a fact of the universe, a resolution of God.

All human history said, "That cannot be." Human nature said, "It can, must, shall." The authors of the American Revolution, as well as the fathers of New England, were transcendentalists to that extent. America had such faith in the idea that she made the experiment in part. She will not quite give up yet. But there is so much of the sensational philosophy in her politics that in half the land the attempt is not made at all, the composite idea is denied, each of the simple ideas is also denied; and in the other half it is but poorly made.

In France men have an idea yet more transcendental; to the intellectual idea of liberty, and the moral idea of equality, they add the religious idea of fraternity, and so put politics and all legislation on a basis divine and incontestable as the truths of mathematics. They say that rights and duties are before all human laws and above all human laws. America says, "The Constitution of the United States is above the President, the Supreme Court above Congress." France says, "The Constitution of the Universe is above the Constitution of France." Forty million people say that. It transcends experience. The grandest thing a nation ever said in history.

The transcendental politician does not say that might makes right, but that there is an immutable morality for nations as for men. Legislation must represent that, or the law is not binding on any man. By birth man is a citizen of the universe, subject to God; no oath of allegiance, no king, no parliament, no congress, no people, can absolve him from his natural fealty thereto, and alienate a man born to the rights, born to the duties, of a citizen of God's universe. Society, government, politics come not from a social compact which men made and may unmake, but from a social nature of God's making; a nation is to be self-ruled by justice. In a monarchy, the king holds power as a trust, not a right: in a democracy, the people have it as a right, the majority as a trust; but the minority have lost no right, can alienate none, delegate none beyond power of ultimate recall. A nation has a right to make just laws, binding because just. Justice is the point common to one man and the world of men, the balance-point. A nation is to seek the greatest good of all, not of the greatest number; not to violate the constitution of the universe, not sacrifice the minority to the majority, nor one single man to the whole. But over all human law God alone has eminent domain.

Here too is a danger: the transcendental politician may seek to ignore the past, and scorn its lessons; may take his own personal whims for oracles of human nature; and so he may take counsel from the selfishness of lazy men against the selfishness of active men, counsel from the selfishness of poor men against the selfishness of rich men, and think he hears the voice of justice, or the reverse, as himself is rich or poor, active or idle; there is danger that he be rash and question as hastily in politics as in physics, and reckon without his host, to find that the scot is not free when the day of reckoning comes.

III. In ethics. Transcendentalism affirms that man has moral faculties which lead him to justice and right, and by his own nature can find out what is right and just, and can know it and be certain of it. Right is to be done come what will come. I am not answerable for the consequences of doing right, only of not doing it, only of doing wrong. The conscience of each man is to him the moral standard; so to mankind is the conscience of the race. In morals conscience is complete and reliable as the eye for colors, the ears for sounds, the touch and taste for their purposes. While experience shows what has been or is, conscience shows what should be and shall.

Transcendental ethics look not to the consequences of virtue, in this life or the next, as motive, therefore, to lead men to virtue. That is itself a good, an absolute good, to be loved not for what it brings, but is. It represents the even poise or balance-point between individual and social development. To know what is right, I need not ask what is the current practice, what say the Revised Statutes, what said holy men of old, but what says conscience? what, God? The common practice, the Revised Statutes, the holy men of old are helps, not masters. I am to be co-ordinate with justice.

Conscience transcends experience, and not only explains but anticipates that, and the transcendental system of morals is to be founded on human nature and absolute justice.

I am to respect my own nature and be an individual man, — your nature and be a social man. Truth is to be told and asked, justice done and demanded, right claimed and allowed, affection felt and received. The will of man is free; not absolutely free as God's, but partially free, and capable of progress to yet higher degrees of freedom.

Do you ask an example of a transcendental moralist? A scheme of morals was once taught to mankind wholly transcendental, the only such scheme that I know. In that was no alloy of expediency, no deference to experience, no crouching behind a fact of human history to hide from ideas of human nature; a scheme of morals which demands that you be you — I, I; balances individualism and socialism on the central point of justice; which puts natural right, natural duty, before all institutions, all laws, all traditions. You will pardon me for mentioning the name of Jesus of Nazareth in a lecture. But the whole of human history did not justify his ethics; only human nature did that. Hebrew ethics, faulty in detail, were worse in method and principle, referring all to an outward command, not an inward law. Heathen ethics less faulty in detail, not less in principles, referred all to experience and expediency, knew only what was, and what worked well here or there; not what ought to be, and worked well anywhere and forever. He transcended that, taught what should be, must, shall, and forever.

The danger is that the transcendental moralist shall too much abhor the actual rules of morality; where much is bad and ill-founded, shall deem all worthless. Danger, too, that he take a transient impulse, personal and fugitive, for a universal law; follow a passion for a principle, and come to naught; surrender his manhood, his free will to his unreflecting instinct, become subordinate thereto. Men that are transcendental-mad we have all seen in morals; to be transcendental-wise, sober, is another thing. The notion that every impulse is to be followed, every instinct totally obeyed, will put man among the beasts, not angels.

IV. In religion. Transcendentalism admits a religious faculty, element, or nature in man, as it admits a moral, intellectual and sensational faculty, — that man by nature is a religious being as well as moral, intellectual, sensational; that this religious faculty is adequate to its purposes and wants, as much so as the others, as the eye acquainting us with light; and that this faculty is the source of religious emotions, of the sentiments of adoration, worship. Through this we have consciousness of God as through the senses consciousness of matter. In connection with reason it gives us the primary ideas of religion, ideas which transcend experience.

Now the transcendental philosophy legitimates the ideas of religion by reference to human nature. Some of them it finds truths of necessity, which cannot be conceived of as false or unreal without violence to reason; some it finds are truths of consciousness, — of spontaneous consciousness, or intuition; some, truths of voluntary consciousness, or demonstration, inductive or deductive. Such ideas, capable of this legitimation, transcend experience, require and admit no further proof; as true before experience as after; true before time, after time, eternally; absolutely true. On that rock transcendentalism founds religion, sees its foundation, and doubts no more of religious truths than of the truths of mathematics. All the truths of religion it finds can be verified in consciousness to-day, what cannot is not religion. But it does not neglect experience. In human history it finds confirmations, illustrations, of the ideas of human nature, for history represents the attempt of mankind to develop human nature. So then as transcendentalism in philosophy legitimates religion by a reference to truths of necessity, to truths of consciousness, it illustrates religion by facts of observation, facts of testimony.

By sensationalism religious faith is a belief, more or less strange, in a probability, a credibility, a possibility. By transcendentalism religious faith is the normal action of the whole spiritual nature of man, which gives him certain knowledge of a certainty not yet attainable by experience; where understanding ends, faith begins, and out-travels the understanding. Religion is natural to man, is justice, piety — free justice, free piety, free thought. The form thereof should fit the individual; hence there will be a unity of substance, diversity of form. So a transcendental religion demands a transcendental theology.

1. The transcendental philosophy appears in its doctrine of God. The idea of God is a fact given in the consciousness of man; consciousness of the infinite is the condition of a consciousness of the finite. I learn of a finite thing by sensation, I get an idea thereof; at the same time the idea of the infinite unfolds in me. I am not conscious of my own existence except as a finite existence, that is, as a dependent existence; and the idea of the infinite, of God on whom I depend, comes at the same time as the logical correlative of a knowledge of myself. So the existence of God is a certainty; I am as certain of that as of my own existence. Indeed without that knowledge I know nothing. Of this I am certain, — I am;

but of this as certain, — God is; for if I am, and am finite and dependent, then this presupposes the infinite and independent. So the idea of God is *a priori;* rests on facts of necessity, on facts of consciousness.

Then transcendentalism uses the other mode, the *a posteriori.* Starting with the infinite, it finds signs and proofs of him everywhere, and gains evidence of God's existence in the limits of sensational observation; the thing refers to its maker, the thought to the mind, the effect to the cause, the created to the creator, the finite to the infinite; at the end of my arms are two major prophets, ten minor prophets, each of them pointing the transcendental philosopher to the infinite God, of which he has consciousness without the logical process of induction.

Then the character of God as given in the idea of him, given in consciousness, — that represents God as a being, not with the limitations of impersonality (that is to confound God with matter); not with the limitations of personality (that confounds him with man); but God with no limitations, infinite, absolute; looked at from sensation, infinite power; from thought, infinite intellect; from the moral sense, infinite conscience; from the emotional, infinite affection; from the religious, infinite soul; from all truth, the whole human nature names him Infinite Father!

God is immanent in matter, so it is; immanent in spirit, so it is. He acts also as God in matter and spirit, acts perfectly; laws of matter or of spirit are modes of God's acting, being; as God is perfect, so the mode of his action is perfect and unchangeable. Therefore, as God is ever in matter and spirit, and where God is is wholly God active, so no intervention is possible. God cannot come where he already is, so no miracle is possible. A miracle *a parte humanâ* is a violation of what is a law to man; a miracle to God — *a parte divinâ* — is a violation of what is law to God: the most extraordinary things that have been seem miracles *a parte humanâ,* — laws, *a parte divinâ.* But though God is immanent in matter and in spirit, he yet transcends both matter and spirit, has no limitations. Indeed all perfection of immanence and transcendence belong to him, — the perfection of existence, infinite being; the perfection of space, immensity; the perfection of time, eternity; of power, all-mightiness; of mind, all-knowingness; of affection, all-lovingness; of will, absolute freedom, absolute justice, absolute right. His providence is not merely general, but universal, so special in each thing. Hence the universe partakes of his perfection, is a perfect universe for the end he made it for.

2. The doctrine of the soul. This teaches that man by nature is immortal. This doctrine it legitimates: 1. By reference to facts of consciousness that men feel in general; in the heart it finds the longing after immortality, in the mind the idea of immortality, in religious consciousness the faith in immortality, in human nature altogether the strong confidence and continued trust therein. 2. It refers also to the nature of God, and reasons thus: God is all-powerful and can do the best; all-wise, and can know it; all-good, and must will it; immortality is the best, therefore it is. All this anticipates experience *a priori.* 3. It refers to the general arrangements of the world, where everything gets ripe, matures, but man. In the history of mankind it finds confirmation of this doctrine, for every rude race and all civilized tribes have been certain of immortality; but here and there are men, sad and unfortunate, who have not by the mind

legitimated the facts of spontaneous consciousness, whose nature the sensational philosophy has made blind, and they doubt or deny what nature spontaneously affirms.

The nature of God being such, he immanent and active in matter and spirit; the nature of man such, so provided with faculties to love the true, the just, the fair, the good, — it follows that man is capable of inspiration from God, communion with God; not in raptures, not by miracle, but by the sober use of all his faculties, moral, intellectual, affectional, religious. The condition thereof is this, the faithful use of human nature, the coincidence of man's will with God's. Inspiration is proportionate to the man's quantity of being, made up of a constant and a variable, his quantity of gifts, his quantity of faithful use. In this way transcendentalism can legitimate the highest inspiration, and explain the genius of God's noblest son, not as monstrous, but natural. In religion as in all things else there has been a progressive development of mankind. The world is a school, prophets, saints, saviours, men more eminently gifted and faithful, and so most eminently inspired, — they are the school-masters to lead men up to God.

There is danger in this matter also lest the transcendental religionist should despise the past and its sober teachings, should take a fancy personal and fugitive for a fact of universal consciousness, embrace a cloud for an angel, and miserably perish. It is not for man to transcend his faculties, to be above himself, above reason, conscience, affection, religious trust. It is easy to turn off from these and be out of reason, conscience, affection, religion — beside himself. Madmen in religion are not rare, enthusiasts, fanatics.

The sensational philosophy, with all its evils, has done the world great service. It has stood up for the body, for common sense, protested against spiritual tyranny, against the spiritualism of the middle ages which thought the senses wicked and the material world profane. To sensationalism we are indebted for the great advance of mankind in physical science, in discovery, arts, mechanics, and for many improvements in government. Some of its men are great names, — Bacon, Locke, Newton. Let us do them no dishonor; they saw what they could, told it; they saw not all things that are, saw some which are not. In our day no one of them would be content with the philosophy they all agreed in then. Hobbes and Hume have done us service; the Socinians, Priestley, Collins, Berkeley, Dodwell, Mandeville, Edwards. To take the good and leave the ill is our part; but the doubts which this philosophy raises, the doubt of Hume, the doubt of Hobbes, of the English Deists in general, do not get answered by this philosophy. For this we have weapons forged by other hands, tempered in another spring.

Transcendentalism has a work to do, to show that physics, politics, ethics, religion rest on facts of necessity, facts of intuition, facts of demonstration, and have their witness and confirmation in facts of observation. It is the work of transcendentalism to give us politics which represent God's thought of a state, — the whole world, each man free; to give us morals which leave the man a complete individual, no chord rent from the human harp, — yet complete in his social character, no string discordant in the social choir; to give us religion worthy of God and man, — free goodness, free piety, free thought. That is not to be done by talking at random, not by idleness, not by railing at authority, calumniating the past or the present; not by idle brains with open mouth, who outrage common sense; but by diligent toil, brave discipline, patience to wait, patience to work. Nothing comes of nothing, foolishness of fools; but something from something, wise thought from thinking men; and of the wise thought comes a lovely deed, life, laws, institutions for mankind.

The problem of transcendental philosophy is no less than this, to revise the experience of mankind and try its teachings by the nature of mankind; to test ethics by conscience, science by reason; to try the creeds of the churches, the constitutions of the states by the constitution of the universe; to reverse what is wrong, supply what is wanting, and command the just. To do this in a nation like ours, blinded still by the sensational philosophy, devoted chiefly to material interests, its politics guided by the madness of party more than sober reason; to do this in a race like the Anglo-Saxon, which has an obstinate leaning to a sensational philosophy, which loves facts of experience, not ideas of consciousness, and believes not in the First-Fair, First-Perfect, First-Good, is no light work; not to be taken in hand by such as cannot bear the strife of tongues, the toil, the heat, the war of thought; not to be accomplished by a single man, however well-born and well-bred; not by a single age and race. It has little of history behind, for this philosophy is young. It looks to a future, a future to be made; a church whose creed is truth, whose worship love; a society full of industry and abundance, full of wisdom, virtue, and the poetry of life; a state with unity among all, with freedom for each; a church without tyranny, a society without ignorance, want, or crime, a state without oppression; yes, a world with no war among the nations to consume the work of their hands, and no restrictive policy to hinder the welfare of mankind. That is the human dream of the transcendental philosophy. Shall it ever become a fact? History says, No; human nature says, Yes.

Henry Steele Commager: THEODORE PARKER

WHAT is a man born for, but to be a reformer. So Emerson had said, and was startled when they took him at his word. Every institution was called before the bar of reason, and of sentiment — the Church, the State, labor, slavery, law and punishment, war, the school, the press, the family. Nothing was taken for granted, nothing but the right of inquiry and the authority of conscience. It was downright uncomfortable to live in Boston in the forties and the fifties; it was not enough that you paid for your pew and stood well in State Street and sent your boys to Harvard College; someone was sure to tell you that the Church was rotten and State Street wicked and that Harvard College taught nothing that a good man need know. Wherever you went the reformers demanded your credentials and your passport, and challenged every signature but their own. Even your private life was not immune; you could not eat or drink in peace but someone would bob up to warn you that to touch meat was a vice and to sip wine a sin.

For the reformers, at least, Boston was the Hub of the Universe. Every town in New England sent its delegate there; they filled the halls with their conventions and the air with their clamor. There was an Aristides at every court, a Diogenes in every countinghouse. Here in this city of the Appletons and the Lees there were as many reformers as there were merchants. Call the roll of the radicals and their names crack out like a volley of musketry: Phillips, Sumner, Garrison, Mann, Quincy, Parker, Pierpont, Channing, Emerson, Alcott, Ripley, Loring, Lowell, Rantoul, Higginson, Howe. No mere fanatics these, no half-baked bedlamites; you could not dismiss a Quincy or a Channing or a Higginson, they were connected with half the families of the State. They could preach pantheism in the pulpit, transcendentalism in the schoolroom, socialism in the market place, abolitionism in Faneuil Hall; they could agitate the most inflammatory of issues, announce the most outlandish ideas, champion the most extravagant causes, and you would have to listen to them. And they consorted with the worst of men, and of women too. Wherever they went they trailed behind them clouds of high-flying enthusiasts — spiritualists, phrenologists, Swedenborgians, Millerites, vegetarians, Grahamites, prohibitionists, feminists, non-resistants, Thomsonians, Come-outers of every shape and every hue.

What had they in common, these reformers, men and women, rich and poor, educated and illiterate? What was it that persuaded Edmund Quincy to preside over the Chardon Street Convention and gave Channing patience to listen to the rantings of Abby Folsom and Syl-

From *Theodore Parker, Yankee Reformer,* by Henry Steele Commager, copyright 1936 by Little, Brown and Company. Reprinted by permission of the author. This extract comprises parts of Chapters 8 and 12.

vanus Brown? What was it that sent Parker and Ripley hot-footing it out to Groton to participate in the wrangling of the Millerites and the Come-outers? What was the magic of Brook Farm that it stirred the hearts of the sanest of men and made them tolerant even of Fruitlands and of Hopedale? Bronson Alcott had made a failure of everything but life, but no matter how fantastic his notions everyone loved him, for he had proved the Dignity of Man. Margaret Fuller was as dangerous as Fanny Wright, but all the women of Boston flocked to her Conversations, and Emerson was glad to contribute to her biography. Horace Mann succumbed to phrenology and Thomas Appleton flirted with spiritualism; Parker was fascinated by mesmerism and Emerson avowed himself a Swedenborgian and took lessons from Sampson Reed. Josiah Quincy thought well of the Mormons and admired Joseph Smith, and Ellis Gray Loring circulated petitions on behalf of Abner Kneeland, who was a convicted atheist and a Thomsonian too. Francis Jackson gave refuge to female abolitionists, Higginson hobnobbed with Lucy Stone and Amelia Bloomer, and Phillips championed the Woman's Movement as the greatest reform in history. Orestes Brownson founded a Society for Christian Progress, Robert Rantoul labored with Seth Parker for the ten-hour day, and John Allen of Brook Farm organized a New England Workingmen's Association, while Channing preached socialism from the pulpit and Parker congratulated the Shakers that they alone had solved the problem of industrialism. Charles Sumner enlisted with Garrison and Elihu Burritt in the war against war, and William Ladd projected a plan for a World Congress of Nations. Pierpont worked for temperance and Neal Dow

for prohibition; wealthy Reverend John Sargent and poor John Augustus tried to stamp out prostitution; Dorothea Dix forced legislatures to ameliorate the lot of the insane, and Samuel Gridley Howe gave light to the blind. Phillips spoke for penal reform and Parker described the criminal as the victim, not the foe, of society, and James Russell Lowell rebuked the aged Wordsworth for his defense of capital punishment: —

And always 'tis the saddest sight to see
An old man faithless in Humanity.

What had they in common — what but a belief in the perfectibility of man and in the doctrine of progress? Emerson had put it well, Emerson who spoke for them, however reluctantly:—"The power which is at once spring and regulator in all efforts of reform is the conclusion that there is an infinite worthiness in man, which will appear at the call of worth, and that all particular reforms are the removing of some impediment." They were all transcendentalists, though they read not Coleridge and knew not Kant. They were all idealists, howsoever they rationalized their emotions or tested them by experience. The ability of man to attain divinity, that was the point of departure. It was assumption, as Rousseau's "Man is born free and is everywhere in chains" was an assumption — as magnificent, as revolutionary in its logical consequences. For if Man is a God, how is it we find him a brute? If man was born free, how is it we find him in spiritual chains? The Calvinists met this issue squarely enough: they rejected the assumptions. But transcendentalists took no stock in Original Sin or the Downfall of Man. They knew that men were born not only free but to the pursuit of happiness, and no matter how sharply Mr. Garrison and Mr. Phillips might take issue with Mr. Parker's theology, they too were transcendentalists at heart.

No need to go to Saint Augustine for the city of God — nor to Fourier, either. No need to escape from reality into the past, or to disown the present and go off by yourself to some Brook Farm or Walden Pond. What better place to build the Heavenly City than here in Boston? And what if the spirit of Hunkerism ruled the town? What if dogma was preached from the pulpits and servility taught in the schools, and one third of the people were from County Cork and went to Mass? What if the merchants built their proud houses on Beacon Hill while the slums grew apace in South Boston and the salt tide flooded the cellars of the ramshackle tenements, bringing disease and death? What if there was a grog shop on every corner and Deer Island was crowded with wretched harlots; what if the law made criminals and then killed them, and Negroes were hunted in the streets of Boston and sent back to the cotton fields of the South? These things did not prove the depravity of Man, for you could not prove an untruth. You could not invalidate a Natural Law by refusing to obey it.

That law was the Law of Progress. Nature and Philosophy united to prove the progress of mankind. Science (not Professor Agassiz's) lent its support, and even history — if you but read it aright — even history demonstrated the sure advance of civilization and the triumph of right over wrong. Theirs was no easy optimism, not the optimism that shaded dangerously into a smug assurance that whatever was, was right, nor yet an optimism so supremely confident of the wisdom of Providence that it faltered

into fatalism. But they read with approval those lines from Locksley Hall —

Yet I doubt not through the ages one increasing purpose runs,
And the thoughts of men are widened with the process of the suns

and felt themselves in tune with the Infinite.

This is what gave them fortitude, the conviction that they were on the side of the angels, that they were fulfilling Nature and Nature's laws, and that the stars in their courses fought for them. This is what gave dignity to their zeal and strength to their numbers. It made them courageous in the face of opposition, resolute in the face of discouragement, eloquent in the face of apathy. It armored them against attack and fortified them against contumely. It gave them a militant, an unconquerable faith, that was at last triumphantly proclaimed by one who knew them all: —

He has sounded forth the trumpet that shall never call retreat;
He is sifting out the hearts of men before His judgment-seat;
O, be swift, my soul, to answer Him! be jubilant, my feet!
Our God is marching on.

God was marching on, but the Church lagged behind. It was, thought Parker, the most conservative of institutions, more concerned with ritual and with dogma than with life. No need to look to the Church for inspiration or support; "even the baby-virtue of America," wrote Parker contemptuously, "turns off from that lean, haggard and empty breast." At the Berry Street Conference Doctor X — remembered how many infants he had baptized that year, and Doctor Y — boasted of the number of tracts they had distributed in the West. At Worcester the Annual Convention argued the terms upon which Persons should be admitted to the Communion and debated the grave question, "Have We a Litany Among Us?"; and in 1853 Doctor Lothrop actually hatched a creed studded with silly phrases about "celestial solicitation" and "the withered veins of humanity." That same year Parker peeped in at the Divinity School and concluded that it was a morgue. "The Egyptian embalmers," he said, "took only seventy days to make a mummy out of a dead man. Unitarian embalmers used three years in making a mummy out of a live one." Doctor Ripley's church looked askance at his ideas of social reform, and Chandler Robbins was proud that no social question had ever intruded itself upon the decorum of his services; the Federal Street Church would not allow Doctor Channing to announce an anti-slavery meeting, and Doctor Frothingham found it hard to understand why anyone should wish to improve a society so nearly perfect. Clergymen stood ready to testify to the good character of a Webster or a Choate, and debated whether Emerson was a Christian; there were separate chapels for the poor, where only the orthodox might preach.

The air of Boston was electric with reform, but the windows of the churches were closed. Yet it was not so elsewhere. Out in Worcester Edward Everett Hale vied with Thomas Wentworth Higginson in the socialization of Christianity; in Syracuse Sam Jo May turned his church over to the radicals; and in New York the talented but eccentric Henry Bellows meddled dangerously with profane affairs. But here in Boston the Unitarians had become respectable and conservative. They were gentlemen and not unaware of the fact; they moved in the

best circles, their conduct was dignified and their manners refined. They worshipped reason and loved peace, and enthusiasm they thought vulgar. Norton was their scholar and James Walker their philosopher, and they read Holmes more gladly than Lowell. There had been liberals in the church, but somehow they had disappeared, and now Doctor Lothrop and Doctor Frothingham set the pace. Pierpont had talked too much, and Sargent had been too independent, and both, now, were gone. Parker himself was outside the pale, and when James Freeman Clarke invited him into his pulpit, his wealthiest parishioners seceded to more comfortable pews. Emerson had left the church; Ripley had left the church; Brownson had left the church. And Channing was gone, Channing whose greatness of spirit had encompassed the town.

Who was there to take the place of Channing? Who was there now to preach the Dignity of Man and the religion of Humanity? He was, thought Parker, the greatest clergyman of his time, the greatest man of his time. For forty years his presence had been a benediction to the city, and his piety an inspiration to the Church. His saintliness was a challenge to sin, and his holiness a rebuke to iniquity. He took the highest ground and drew men to him; he made the most audacious assumptions and shamed men into granting them. His idealism was inexorable, his faith in the goodness of man was not to be gainsaid, and when men disappointed him, his grief stung them like conscience. He had not great learning, but he spoke with the authority of law; he had neither brilliance nor wit, but his words flew around the earth.

No one had achieved more for reform than had Channing, who was not afraid to descend from seraphic abstractions to homely applications. He had the innocence of Alcott, but he did not suffer fools gladly nor live in a world of his own imagining; he had the serenity of Emerson, but he was not willing to adjourn the present for the future or to insist upon the proper limits of his own responsibility. His tolerance did not paralyze his moral sensibilities nor his magnanimity cool his passion for righteousness. He made heresy plausible and revolution respectable; he lent dignity to every reform, and clothed the most dangerous doctrines in the garments of gentility.

With every year he grew more radical in his thinking and bolder in his action. The Peace Society of Massachusetts was organized in his study; and in his study, too, Dorothea Dix prepared her moving Memorial on the condition of the insane. He championed penal reform and the abolition of capital punishment, and assured his wealthy parishioners that the criminal caught the infection of vice from the upper classes. He was among the first to celebrate the work of Horace Mann, and he urged the President of Harvard College to provide democratic education for the plain people of the country. He gave his name to a form of Unitarianism, but he had no proprietary interest in the Church and he was more afraid of conformity than of dissent. He supported Father Taylor and encouraged Brownson and welcomed James Freeman Clarke, and at his death the Catholic Church honored the man who had befriended Bishop Cheverus. When Abner Kneeland was jugged for blasphemy, it was Channing who drew up the petition for pardon; when Faneuil Hall was denied to the abolitionists, it was Channing who secured it for them by his Appeal to the Citizens of Boston. He did not fail to

countenance by his presence the Chardon Street Convention, and from the platform of Faneuil Hall he denounced the murderers of Elijah Lovejoy. "I have no fear of revolutions," he said, "we have conservative principles enough." He was not a socialist, but no Brook Farmer could have condemned more severely the sins of property; he was not a non-resistant, but no pacifist could have painted more blackly the degradation of war; he was not an abolitionist, but his objections to slavery had carried conviction where Garrison's did not. He was independent of every reform group, but aloof from none; he belonged to no clique but gave strength to them all. He was a leader and a symbol, and now he was gone there was none to take his place. . . .

So Parker came in to join the Boston reformers, to make his peculiar contribution of applied Christianity. His church had been organized just for him, and under no ordinary auspices, and something more was expected than a performance of ritual or an annotation of the Gospels. Not because of his learning or his eloquence, or even his piety, had it been resolved "that the Rev. Theodore Parker shall have a chance to be heard in Boston," but because he was the one spokesman of transcendentalism among the clergy, the one uncompromising critic of Hunkerism in the Church. No one else could do what he was expected to do, not James Freeman Clarke, not Pierpont, nor Sargent, nor young Starr King, for all their good intentions. Among all the Boston clergy Parker was the only one to associate on equal terms with the lay reformers, with Garrison and Mann, Phillips and Howe. And among all the reformers, he was the only one who found it possible to remain in the Church and to use the pulpit as the vantage ground from which to direct the attack. He had seen the Church become the apologist for the established order, he had seen the leadership in moral progress pass from the clergy to the laity; he remained stubbornly convinced that the Church might yet be made an instrument for social reform, and he was bold enough to assume responsibility for the experiment. He was not a Channing, but he hoped to complete what Channing had inaugurated. Did he anticipate, that winter day of 1846 when he conducted his own installation as Minister of the Twenty-eighth Congregational Society, did he anticipate that preëminence which was to bring him such odium as no other clergyman suffered, such honor as no other clergyman knew, that fame which was to make his name a byword and a benediction? Did he foresee the strange company he was to keep in the coming years, the peculiar causes he was to plead, the power he was to wield? "I did not know what was latent in myself," he wrote years later, "nor foresee all the doctrines which then were hid in my own first principles, what embryo fruit and flowers lay sheathed in the obvious bud." Yet all the future was implicit in that installation sermon on *The True Idea of the Christian Church.*

"A Christian Church," he said, standing there so young and so terribly earnest, so anxious to do justice to his theme and to reach the hearts of the hundreds who had crowded into the great Melodeon, — "A Christian Church should be the means of reforming the world, of forming it after the pattern of Christian ideas. It should therefore bring up the sentiments of the times, the ideas of the times, and the actions of the times, to judge them by the universal standard. We expect the sins of commerce to be winked at in the streets; the sins of the state to be applauded on election day and in a Congress, or on the Fourth of July; we are used to hear them called the righteousness of the nation. You expect them to be tried by passion, which looks only to immediate results and partial ends. Here they are to be measured by Conscience and Reason, which look to permanent results and universal ends; to be looked at with reference to the Laws of God, the everlasting ideas on which alone is based the welfare of the world. If the church be true, many things which seem gainful in the street and expedient in the senate-house, will here be set down as wrong, and all gain which comes therefrom seem to be but a loss. If there be a public sin in the land, if a lie invade the state, it is for the church to give the alarm; it is here that it may war on lies and sin; the more widely they are believed in and practised, the more are they deadly, the more to be opposed. Here let no false idea or false action of the public go without exposure or rebuke. But let no noble heroism of the times, no noble man pass by without due honor."

Nothing was beyond the province of the Church, nothing foreign to its interest or exempt from its control. Its jurisdiction embraced the morals of the State as well as the morals of men, its purpose was the salvation of society as well as the salvation of the individual. Its liturgy was social welfare, its sacraments good works, its creed the perfectibility of man. It was Catholic in its authority, Protestant in its attitude. There was no responsibility it could evade, no duty it could ignore. Every beggar, every pauper, was a reproach, every poorhouse, every jail, a disgrace, and it was hypocrisy to pretend to a religion of love and tolerate the injustices of man to man. For nineteen centuries the Church had preached the doctrine of Brotherly Love; how could it explain the persistence of brutal crime and vengeful punishment, of iniquity committed in the name of Property, and murder sanctioned by the State? Too long had the Church been silent in the face of these evils, too long concerned with dogma and sectarian strife, too long the refuge of the powerful and the sanctuary of the strong. What, indeed, had the Church been doing all this time that the almshouses were crowded and the jails full and harlots walked the streets of Boston? What had the Church been doing that slavery was tolerated and war glorified and labor exploited and woman oppressed and the rich suffered to lord it over the poor? What had the Church been doing that the blind were denied light, and the feeble-minded treated like animals, and children allowed to grow up in ignorance and want, toiling long hours in the factories and going to school in crime? "If the church were to waste less time in building its palaces of theological speculation, palaces mainly of straw, and based upon the chaff, it would surely have more time to use in the practical good works of the day."

This was the heroism of the present, the sainthood of the future, not the defense of a creed or the punishment of a heresy, but the philanthropy that toiled for the ignorant and the needy, for the vagrant and the drunkard, the prostitute and the thief. No need for the Church to seek refuge in abstractions, to preach nebulous moral sentiments; here was work enough at hand, here were causes to enlist the energies of every Christian. War against the crime of war, war against the crime of slavery, war against intemperance and vice, against poverty and ignorance and disease. Of what

value the triumph of science and of the arts, if morals lag behind? But apply religion to life, sincerely, intelligently, and you could make over society, you could work a real revolution. "We should build up a great state where there was an honorable work for every hand, bread for all mouths, clothing for all backs, culture for every mind, and love and faith in every heart. . . . The noblest monument to Christ, the fairest trophy of religion, is a noble people, where all are well fed and clad, industrious, free, educated, manly, pious, wise and good."

Here was a confession of faith for the church militant, here was a program of practical philanthropy, a pledge for reform. Let no one mistake the purpose for which the Twenty-eighth Congregational Society had been organized, let no one misapprehend the philosophy which inspired its minister. He was done, now, with theological polemics, done with bickering over a Unitarian creed or quarreling over the privilege of an exchange. He had formulated the Articles of Faith; now for a Sacrament of Works. . . .

When it was the Slave Power crowding Kansas with Border Ruffians or striking down Sumner in his Senate seat, Parker was sure that that South was desperate, and he wrote "The Devil is in great wrath because he knoweth that his time is short." Was the North, too, in despair, that it had to resort to Sharpes rifles and to massacre in Potawatomi and that good men applauded the raid on Harper's Ferry? Parker did not really face this question. The aggressions of freedom, he felt, were justified by a different philosophy. These things were no confessions of moral bankruptcy, as with the South. It was not that John Brown's way was the only way. Neither persuasion nor politics had been abandoned, this was merely another expedient: if the South could not understand Garrison or Sumner, perhaps it could learn to understand men like John Brown. "We want all sorts of weapons to attack slavery with," Parker wrote to Thayer, when that deluded philanthropist proposed the colonization of the South itself, "the heavy artillery and the light horse which cuts the lines asunder and routs a whole column before they know the enemy is upon them."

He was convinced that only war could settle this matter of slavery, but he did not embrace a foolish consistency and abdicate politics. He was convinced that the Union would not hold together, but he would not go along with Garrison and Phillips in working for its dissolution, not as long as four million Negroes were slaves. War would come, there was no doubt of it; he had been predicting it ever since the Compromise, and because he was so sure of it, he helped to bring it on. He preached the inevitable conflict, he talked of appealing from the parchment of the Constitution to the parchment on the head of a drum, he struck fine gestures and assured his friends that he bought no more books — he needed his money for cannon.

War would come, and within a few years, too, but sufficient unto the day was the evil thereof, and meantime there was some hope in politics. "I think we live in a time when it is a man's *Duty* to attend to political affairs," he had written, and he was never one to neglect his Duty. He was up to his neck in politics, now, and he fancied himself a power behind the scenes; he took himself seriously and he was taken seriously. He went barnstorming around the country and men forgot his heterodoxy and listened to his politics; only Beecher could

command a greater audience, only Greeley was more widely read. His acquaintance was immense, it embraced all of the radical politicians of the North, and he did not hesitate to presume upon it. Not since the days of the Puritan theocracy had any clergyman used so lordly a tone. He knew the place of religion and of politics; he knew that it is less worthy to serve Cæsar than to serve God. He could tell all the politicians what to do and ignore the consequences; what had he to do with consequences? When Sumner was elected to the Senate, Parker sat down and wrote him a letter.

You told me once that you were in morals, not in politics. Now I hope you will show that you are still in morals, although in politics. I hope you will be the *senator with a conscience*. I expect you to make mistakes, blunders; but I hope they will be intellectual and not moral; that you will never miss the Right, however you may miss the Expedient ... I hope you will build on the Rock of Ages, and look to eternity for your justification. You see, my dear Sumner, that I expect much of you, that I expect heroism of the most heroic kind. The moral and manly excellence of all our prominent men is greatly over-rated by the mass of men. You see I try you by a difficult standard and that I am not easily pleased.

And Sumner, the proud Sumner, humorless and didactic, listened courteously to this sermon (he was used to sermons, he wrote them himself), and tried to be the *senator with a conscience*.

When Wilson went to the Senate, Wilson, the Natick cobbler who justified democracy, Parker warned him that he think more of principles and less of political advancement: —

There is only one thing which made me prefer Charles Francis Adams or S. C. Phillips to you. You have been seeking for office with all your might. Now I don't like this hunting for office in foes and still less in my friends. But for this you would have been my first choice for the senatorship . . . Now let me tell you what I think are the dangers of your position, and also what noble things I expect of you.

And Wilson, who was to disappoint so often those expectations, answered meekly: "I sometimes read over the letter you were so kind as to send me. You dealt frankly with me in that letter, and I thank you for it, and I hope to be better and wiser for it. I shall endeavor while in the Senate to act up to my convictions of duty, to do what I feel to be right." But it was not enough, and soon Sumner had to intercede for Wilson: "I fear you are too harsh upon Wilson, and I fear that you and others will help undermine him by furnishing arguments to the lukewarm and the Hunkers. Bear this in mind and be gentle."

But it was not in Parker to be gentle when moral issues were at stake, and Sumner himself was to feel the flick of his whip more than once. "I thought you did not quite do your duty in 1850–51," Parker wrote him, and when he did not speak at Parker's bidding, Mason of Virginia taunted him: "I see my friend Theodore Parker is after you." And so he was, letter after letter, egging him on, and to Howe, "Do you see what imminent deadly peril poor Sumner is in? If he does not speak, he is *dead — dead — dead.*" But Sumner was not dead, and soon he found an opportunity to make the speech that was expected of him, and Parker was quick to write his approval — and careful to qualify it. "You have made a grand speech," he assured the Senator. "It was worth while to go to Congress to make such a speech. You have done

what I have all along said you would do, though I lamented that you did not do it long ago." But there was mutual respect behind all of this, and affection too, and when Sumner was assaulted by Brooks, none grieved more deeply than Parker. "I wish that I could have taken the blows on my head," he wrote, but his sympathy for his friend did not becloud his understanding of the significance of the attack. "Slave holders are not fools," he pointed out. "The South never struck down a Northern advocate of a tariff or a defender of the Union. It attacks only the soldiers of freedom, knowing that the controlling power of the North also hates them."

Sumner and Wilson were Parker's Senators, and he had a right to counsel them, but he did not confine himself to the Senators from Massachusetts: he was father-confessor and spiritual adviser to all the leaders of the Free Soil and Republican parties. Did Seward understand the situation, Seward, whom he was grooming for the Presidency? "Dear Sir," Parker wrote him, "It seems to me that the country has got now to such a pass that the people must interfere and take things out of the hands of the politicians who now control them. Allow me to show *in extenso* what I mean."

And he did, in one long letter after another, and soon Seward was in Boston, canvassing the political situation with Parker, and on his return to Washington he wrote: "I assured Mr. Sumner and Mr. Wilson that I considered Massachusetts at least organized to the cause of Human Nature. In my own thoughts I have constantly supposed that consummation if speedily attained, was to be due to your restless and sagacious and vigorous ability." And when Parker came to New York he told his audience, "There is not at this day a politician so able, so

far-sighted, so cautious, so wise, so dis-
criminating, as William Henry Seward,"
— and this even though Mr. Seward had
"no drop of Puritan blood in his veins."

With Chase he was on a more familiar
footing. "What a noble man Chase is,"
Parker exclaimed. "He called to see me
yesterday. His face is a benediction to
any audience; what a fine eye he has."
And to Chase himself: "I *do* consider
you a great man and a great statesman.
If you are not a great statesman, then
who is?" Chase could not answer this
question, but, not to be outdone, he assured Parker: "I always like to read your
heroic utterances." But their relations
were not always on this idyllic plane.
When Chase failed to rescue the poor
fugitive Margaret Garner, Parker tore
into him: "I thought the anti-slavery
Governor of Ohio would get possession
of that noble woman, either by the hocus-
pocus of some legal technicality, or else
by the *red right arm of Ohio,* and I confess that I was terribly chagrined that it
did not turn out so." And he went on to
New York and told his audience there,
"If three and a half millions of slaves
had been white men, do you suppose the
affair at Cincinnati would have turned
out after that sort? Do you suppose
Governor Chase would have said, 'No
slavery outside of the slave States, but
inside of the slave States, just as much
enslavement of Anglo-Saxon men as you
please'?" Chase hadn't said any such
thing, and he did not hesitate to tell
Parker so, and to tell him how wrong he
was in this and in other matters. Was
Parker disposed to criticize his conduct?
He was not satisfied with Parker's conduct, either, and sometimes Parker threw
him into despair by his willful intermix-
ing of religious with political radicalism.
"Shall I not say to you frankly," Chase
wrote, "how much I regret that on the

great question of the Divine Origin of
the Bible and the Divine Nature of Christ
your views are so little in harmony with
those of almost all who labour with you
in the great cause of Human Enfran-
chisement and Progress." Yet their friendship weathered these recriminations.
When Chase came to Boston he did not
fail to attend the Music Hall, however
much he disapproved of the theology
which he heard there, and when Parker
invaded Ohio he visited the Governor in
Columbus and saw his own picture hang-
ing in the dining room and his sermons
lying on the table of the Executive Office.

He knew them all and he made his
influence felt. He could see things that
the politicians could not see, for he was
a philosopher; he could say things that
the politicians could not say, for he had
no career to consider. "The non-political
reformer," he pointed out, "is not re-
stricted by any law, any Constitution,
any man, nor by the people, because he
is not to deal with institutions; he is to
make the institutions better. The non-
political reformer is to raise the cotton,
to spin it into thread, to weave it into
web, to prescribe the pattern after which
the dress is to be made; and then he is
to pass the cloth and the pattern to the
political reformer, and say 'Now, Sir,
take your shears, and cut it out and make
it up.'" Easy enough for Parker, he was
good at spinning thread and weaving
webs, and better still at prescribing the
patterns for the politicians to cut. "Now
a word about Kansas . . ." he would write
to Senator Hale, and there would follow
pages of illegible manuscript for Mr.
Hale to decipher. And, "now *my* way of
dealing with the nation is this . . ." he
would inform Governor Banks (a broken
reed, this Banks) and there would be a
long disquisition on the character of a
political party and the duty of the Re-

publicans to abolish slavery everywhere. Or to William Herndon on the Ottawa debate: "Mr. Lincoln did not meet the issue. He made a technical evasion. That is not the way to fight the battle of Freedom." Parker knew how to fight the battle of Freedom, and he lectured them all on grand strategy and on tactics — Bancroft and Birney, Palfrey and Mann, Adams and Julian, as well as the great leaders of the party. "Among all my old friends, there is not one that I can consult with the same confidence I can you," Birney assured him; and from Herndon came a letter to Lydia, "He is about the only man living who can hold me steady."

But it was not all a matter of writing letters or of preaching sermons. He tried his hand at practical politics; in '54 he was busy getting up a convention of all the Free States, and the next year he was circulating petitions throughout the North for the removal of those Federal Judges who had ruled wrongly on the Fugitive Slave Bill. When Sumner was attacked, Parker told Hale, "I shall go to the State House as soon as the House meets to see if I can stir up that body to action," and when the Republicans declared that it was not their intention to attack slavery in the States, he wrote, "It is *my* intention as soon as I get the power." His study was a clearinghouse of radical opinion; here men like Chase and Hale could find out for themselves how relevant were the arguments of Garrison and Phillips. Parker knew what was going on in every State, and everywhere he held up the hands of the radicals and cried down compromise. A political realist, he saw the economic bases of politics; an idealist, he refused to recognize them or to accommodate himself to them. He knew that the Whig Party was no less subservient to vested interests than was the Democratic Party to slavery, and he warned his friends of the attempt of the money power to get control of the new Republican Party. He saw even the effect of the new railroads upon the struggle for freedom in the West, but his perspicuity did not lure him into the compromise fatal to Rantoul, nor bring him over to Douglas, and his abiding fear of that statesman was not without effect in heading off the consummation of Greeley's plot to swing the Little Giant over into the Republican Party.

How much influence did Parker exert, after all? Did Sumner need his prodding or Hale his encouragement? Did Seward benefit by his advice, did Chase profit by his warnings? The task of the nonpolitical reformer, he had said, was to create sentiment, to advance ideas, to suggest modes of action. He had stirred up sentiment enough, and he was generous with ideas, but the only mode of action he could suggest, in the end, was agitation, and that led to war, which is what the politicians were trying to avoid. Yet it was something to be in advance of the politicians without breaking the lines of communication as Garrison had broken them. It was something to rebuke timidity and reject compromise and formulate a policy of aggression, to recall men to fundamental principles and denounce a policy of expediency. It was something to be the Conscience of a Party.

Louisa May Alcott: TRANSCENDENTAL WILD OATS – A Chapter from an Unwritten Romance

ON the first day of June, 184–, a large wagon, drawn by a small horse and containing a motley load, went lumbering over certain New England hills, with the pleasing accompaniments of wind, rain, and hail. A serene man with a serene child upon his knee was driving, or rather being driven, for the small horse had it all his own way. A brown boy with a William Penn style of countenance sat beside him, firmly embracing a bust of Socrates. Behind them was an energetic-looking woman, with a benevolent brow, satirical mouth, and eyes brimful of hope and courage. A baby reposed upon her lap, a mirror leaned against her knee, and a basket of provisions danced about at her feet, as she struggled with a large, unruly umbrella. Two blue-eyed little girls, with hands full of childish treasures, sat under one old shawl, chatting happily together.

In front of this lively party stalked a tall, sharp-featured man, in a long blue cloak; and a fourth small girl trudged along beside him through the mud as if she rather enjoyed it.

The wind whistled over the bleak hills; the rain fell in a despondent drizzle, and twilight began to fall. But the calm man gazed as tranquilly into the fog as if he beheld a radiant bow of promise spanning the gray sky. The cheery woman tried to cover every one but herself with the big umbrella. The brown boy pillowed his head on the bald pate of Socrates and slumbered peacefully. The little girls sang lullabies to their dolls in soft, maternal murmurs. The sharp-nosed pedestrian marched steadily on, with the blue cloak streaming out behind him like a banner; and the lively infant splashed through the puddles with a ducklike satisfaction pleasant to behold.

Thus these modern pilgrims journeyed hopefully out of the old world, to found a new one in the wilderness.

The editors of *The Transcendental Tripod* had received from Messrs. Lion & Lamb (two of the aforesaid pilgrims) a communication from which the following statement is an extract: –

"We have made arrangements with the proprietor of an estate of about a hundred acres which liberates this tract from human ownership. Here we shall prosecute our effort to initiate a Family in harmony with the primitive instincts of man.

"Ordinary secular farming is not our object. Fruit, grain, pulse, herbs, flax, and other vegetable products, receiving

From *Silver Pitchers* (1876). The names used in this sketch of the Fruitlands utopia are fictional. They correspond to the following actual names: Abel Lamb and Sister Hope, Amos Bronson Alcott and Mrs. Alcott; Timon Lion, Charles Lane, Alcott's English admirer; John Pease, Samuel Bower; Forest Absalom, Abram Everett; Moses White, Joseph Palmer, "the man with the beard"; Jane Gage, Anna Page.

assiduous attention, will afford ample manual occupation, and chaste supplies for the bodily needs. It is intended to adorn the pastures with orchards, and to supersede the labor of cattle by the spade and the pruning-knife.

"Consecrated to human freedom, the land awaits the sober culture of devoted men. Beginning with small pecuniary means, this enterprise must be rooted in a reliance on the succors of an ever-bounteous Providence, whose vital affinities being secured by this union with un-corrupted field and unworldly persons, the cares and injuries of a life of gain are avoided.

"The inner nature of each member of the Family is at no time neglected. Our plan contemplates all such disciplines, cultures, and habits as evidently conduce to the purifying of the inmates.

"Pledged to the spirit alone, the founders anticipate no hasty or numerous addition to their numbers. The kingdom of peace is entered only through the gates of self-denial; and felicity is the test and the reward of loyalty to the un-swerving law of Love."

This prospective Eden at present consisted of an old red farm-house, a dilapidated barn, many acres of meadow-land, and a grove. Ten ancient apple-trees were all the "chaste supply" which the place offered as yet; but, in the firm belief that plenteous orchards were soon to be evoked from their inner conscious-ness, these sanguine founders had chris-tened their domain Fruitlands.

Here Timon Lion intended to found a colony of Latter Day Saints, who, under his patriarchal sway, should re-generate the world and glorify his name for ever. Here Abel Lamb, with the devoutest faith in the high ideal which was to him a living truth, desired to plant a Paradise, where Beauty, Virtue, Jus-tice, and Love might live happily to-gether, without the possibility of a ser-pent entering in. And here his wife, unconverted but faithful to the end, hoped, after many wanderings over the face of the earth, to find rest for herself and a home for her children.

"There is our new abode," announced the enthusiast, smiling with a satisfac-tion quite undamped by the drops drip-ping from his hat-brim, as they turned at length into a cart-path that wound along a steep hillside into a barren-looking valley.

"A little difficult of access," observed his practical wife, as she endeavored to keep her various household gods from going overboard with every lurch of the laden ark.

"Like all good things. But those who earnestly desire and patiently seek will soon find us," placidly responded the phi-losopher from the mud, through which he was now endeavoring to pilot the much-enduring horse.

"Truth lies at the bottom of a well, Sister Hope," said Brother Timon, paus-ing to detach his small comrade from a gate, whereon she was perched for a clearer gaze into futurity.

"That's the reason we so seldom get at it, I suppose," replied Mrs. Hope, making a vain clutch at the mirror, which a sudden jolt sent flying out of her hands.

"We want no false reflections here," said Timon, with a grim smile, as he crunched the fragments under foot in his onward march.

Sister Hope held her peace, and looked wistfully through the mist at her prom-ised home. The old red house with a hospitable glimmer at its windows cheered her eyes; and, considering the weather, was a fitter refuge than the sylvan bowers some of the more ardent souls might have preferred.

The new-comers were welcomed by one of the elect precious, — a regenerate farmer, whose idea of reform consisted chiefly in wearing white cotton raiment and shoes of untanned leather. This costume, with a snowy beard, gave him a venerable, and at the same time a somewhat bridal appearance.

The goods and chattels of the Society not having arrived, the weary family reposed before the fire on blocks of wood, while Brother Moses White regaled them with roasted potatoes, brown bread and water, in two plates, a tin pan, and one mug; his table service being limited. But, having cast the forms and vanities of a depraved world behind them, the elders welcomed hardship with the enthusiasm of new pioneers, and the children heartily enjoyed this foretaste of what they believed was to be a sort of perpetual picnic.

During the progress of this frugal meal, two more brothers appeared. One was a dark, melancholy man, clad in homespun, whose peculiar mission was to turn his name hind part before and use as few words as possible. The other was a bland, bearded Englishman, who expected to be saved by eating uncooked food and going without clothes. He had not yet adopted the primitive costume, however; but contented himself with meditatively chewing dry beans out of a basket.

"Every meal should be a sacrament, and the vessels used should be beautiful and symbolical," observed Brother Lamb, mildly, righting the tin pan slipping about on his knees. "I priced a silver service when in town, but it was too costly; so I got some graceful cups and vases of Britannia ware."

"Hardest things in the world to keep bright. Will whiting be allowed in the community?" inquired Sister Hope, with a housewife's interest in labor-saving institutions.

"Such trivial questions will be discussed at a more fitting time," answered Brother Timon, sharply, as he burnt his fingers with a very hot potato. "Neither sugar, molasses, milk, butter, cheese, nor flesh are to be used among us, for nothing is to be admitted which has caused wrong or death to man or beast."

"Our garments are to be linen till we learn to raise our own cotton or some substitute for woolen fabrics," added Brother Abel, blissfully basking in an imaginary future as warm and brilliant as the generous fire before him.

"Haou abaout shoes?" asked Brother Moses, surveying his own with interest.

"We must yield that point till we can manufacture an innocent substitute for leather. Bark, wood, or some durable fabric will be invented in time. Meanwhile, those who desire to carry out our idea to the fullest extent can go barefooted," said Lion, who liked extreme measures.

"I never will, nor let my girls," murmured rebellious Sister Hope, under her breath.

"Haou do you cattle'ate to treat the ten-acre lot? Ef things ain't 'tended to right smart, we shan't hev no crops," observed the practical patriarch in cotton.

"We shall spade it," replied Abel, in such perfect good faith that Moses said no more, though he indulged in a shake of the head as he glanced at hands that had held nothing heavier than a pen for years. He was a paternal old soul and regarded the younger men as promising boys on a new sort of lark.

"What shall we do for lamps, if we cannot use any animal substance? I do hope light of some sort is to be thrown upon the enterprise," said Mrs. Lamb, with anxiety, for in those days kerosene and camphene were not, and gas unknown in the wilderness.

"We shall go without till we have discovered some vegetable oil or wax to to serve us," replied Brother Timon, in a decided tone, which caused Sister Hope to resolve that her private lamp should be always trimmed, if not burning.

"Each member is to perform the work for which experience, strength, and taste best fit him," continued Dictator Lion. "Thus drudgery and disorder will be avoided and harmony prevail. We shall rise at dawn, begin the day by bathing, followed by music, and then a chaste repast of fruit and bread. Each one finds congenial occupation till the meridian meal; when some deep-searching conversation gives rest to the body and development to the mind. Healthful labor again engages us till the last meal, when we assemble in social communion, prolonged till sunset, when we retire to sweet repose, ready for the next day's activity."

"What part of the work do you incline to yourself?" asked Sister Hope, with a humorous glimmer in her keen eyes.

"I shall wait till it is made clear to me. Being in preference to doing is the great aim, and this comes to us rather by a resigned willingness than a wilful activity, which is a check to all divine growth," responded Brother Timon.

"I thought so." And Mrs. Lamb sighed audibly, for during the year he had spent in her family Brother Timon had so faithfully carried out his idea of "being, not doing," that she had found his "divine growth" both an expensive and unsatisfactory process.

Here her husband struck into the conversation, his face shining with the light and joy of the splendid dreams and high ideals hovering before him.

"In these steps of reform, we do not rely so much on scientific reasoning or physiological skill as on the spirit's dictates. The greater part of man's duty consists in leaving alone much that he now does. Shall I stimulate with tea, coffee, or wine? No. Shall I consume flesh? Not if I value health. Shall I subjugate cattle? Shall I claim property in any created thing? Shall I trade? Shall I adopt a form of religion? Shall I interest myself in politics? To how many of these questions — could we ask them deeply enough and could they be heard as having relation to our eternal welfare — would the response be 'Abstain'?"

A mild snore seemed to echo the last word of Abel's rhapsody, for Brother Moses had succumbed to mundane slumber and sat nodding like a massive ghost. Forest Absalom, the silent man, and John Pease, the English member, now departed to the barn; and Mrs. Lamb led her flock to a temporary fold, leaving the founders of the "Consociate Family" to build castles in the air till the fire went out and the symposium ended in smoke.

The furniture arrived next day, and was soon bestowed; for the principal property of the community consisted in books. To this rare library was devoted the best room in the house, and the few busts and pictures that still survived many flittings were added to beautify the sanctuary, for here the family was to meet for amusement, instruction, and worship.

Any housewife can imagine the emotions of Sister Hope, when she took possession of a large, dilapidated kitchen, containing an old stove and the peculiar stores out of which food was to be evolved for her little family of eleven. Cakes of maple sugar, dried peas and beans, barley and hominy, meal of all sorts, potatoes, and dried fruit. No milk, butter, cheese, tea, or meat appeared. Even salt was considered a useless luxury and spice entirely forbidden by these lovers of Spartan simplicity. A ten years' experience of vegetarian vagaries had been good training for this new freak, and her sense of the ludicrous supported her through many trying scenes.

Unleavened bread, porridge, and water for breakfast; bread, vegetables, and water for dinner; bread, fruit, and water for supper was the bill of fare ordained by the elders. No teapot profaned that sacred stove, no gory steak cried aloud for vengeance from her chaste gridiron; and only a brave woman's taste, time, and temper were sacrificed on that domestic altar.

The vexed question of light was settled by buying a quantity of bayberry wax for candles; and, on discovering that no one knew how to make them, pine knots were introduced, to be used when absolutely necessary. Being summer, the evenings were not long, and the weary fraternity found it no great hardship to retire with the birds. The inner light was sufficient for most of them. But Mrs. Lamb rebelled. Evening was the only time she had to herself, and while the tired feet rested the skilful hands mended torn frocks and little stockings, or anxious heart forgot its burden in a book.

So "mother's lamp" burned steadily, while the philosophers built a new heaven and earth by moonlight; and through all the metaphysical mists and philanthropic pyrotechnics of that period Sister Hope played her own little game of "throwing light," and none but the moths were the worse for it.

Such farming probably was never seen before since Adam delved. The band of brothers began by spading garden and field; but a few days of it lessened their ardor amazingly. Blistered hands and aching backs suggested the expediency of permitting the use of cattle till the workers were better fitted for noble toil by a summer of the new life.

Brother Moses brought a yoke of oxen from his farm, — at least, the philosophers thought so till it was discovered that one of the animals was a cow; and Moses confessed that he "must be let down easy, for he couldn't live on garden sarse entirely."

Great was Dictator Lion's indignation at this lapse from virtue. But time pressed, the work must be done; so the meek cow was permitted to wear the yoke and the recreant brother continued to enjoy forbidden draughts in the barn, which dark proceeding caused the children to regard him as one set apart for destruction.

The sowing was equally peculiar, for, owing to some mistake, the three brethren, who devoted themselves to this graceful task, found when about half through the job that each had been sowing a different sort of grain in the same field; a mistake which caused much perplexity, as it could not be remedied; but, after a long consultation and a good deal of laughter, it was decided to say nothing and see what would come of it.

The garden was planted with a generous supply of useful roots and herbs; but, as manure was not allowed to profane the virgin soil, few of these vegetable treasures ever came up. Purslane reigned supreme, and the disappointed planters ate it philosophically, deciding that Nature knew what was best for them, and would generously supply their needs, if they could only learn to digest her "sallets" and wild roots.

The orchard was laid out, a little grafting done, new trees and vines set, regardless of the unfit season and entire ignorance of the husbandmen, who honestly believed that in the autumn they would reap a bounteous harvest.

Slowly things got into order, and rapidly rumors of the new experiment went abroad, causing many strange spirits to flock thither, for in those days communities were the fashion and transcendentalism raged wildly. Some came to look on and laugh, some to be supported in poetic idleness, a few to believe sincerely and work heartily. Each member was allowed to mount his favorite hobby and ride it to his heart's content. Very queer were some of the riders, and very rampant some of the hobbies.

One youth, believing that language was of little consequence if the spirit was only right, startled new-comers by blandly greeting them with "Good-morning, damn you," and other remarks of an equally mixed order. A second irrepressible being held that all the emotions of the soul should be freely expressed, and illustrated his theory by antics that would have sent him to a lunatic asylum, if, as an unregenerate wag said, he had not already been in one. When his spirit soared, he climbed trees and shouted; when doubt assailed him, he lay upon the floor and groaned lamentably. At joyful periods, he raced, leaped, and sang; when sad, he wept aloud; and when a great thought burst upon him in the watches of the night, he crowed like a jocund cockerel, to the great delight of the children and the great annoyance of the elders. One musical brother fiddled whenever so moved, sang sentimentally to the four little girls, and put a music-box on the wall when he hoed corn.

Brother Pease ground away at his uncooked food, or browsed over the farm on sorrel, mint, green fruit, and new vegetables. Occasionally he took his walks abroad, airily attired in an unbleached cotton *poncho,* which was the nearest approach to the primeval costume he was allowed to indulge in. At midsummer he retired to the wilderness, to try his plan where the woodchucks were without prejudices and huckleberry-bushes were hospitably full. A

sunstroke unfortunately spoilt his plan, and he returned to semi-civilization a sadder and wiser man.

Forest Absalom preserved his Pythagorean silence, cultivated his fine dark locks, and worked like a beaver, setting an excellent example of brotherly love, justice, and fidelity by his upright life. He it was who helped overworked Sister Hope with her heavy washes, kneaded the endless succession of batches of bread, watched over the children, and did the many tasks left undone by the brethren, who were so busy discussing and defining great duties that they forgot to perform the small ones.

Moses White placidly plodded about, "chorin' raound," as he called it, looking like an old-time patriarch, with his silver hair and flowing beard, and saving the community from many a mishap by his thrift and Yankee shrewdness.

Brother Lion domineered over the whole concern; for, having put the most money into the speculation, he was resolved to make it pay, — as if anything founded on an ideal basis could be expected to do so by any but enthusiasts.

Abel Lamb simply revelled in the Newness, firmly believing that his dream was to be beautifully realized and in time not only little Fruitlands, but the whole earth, be turned into a Happy Valley. He worked with every muscle of his body, for *he* was in deadly earnest. He taught with his whole head and heart; planned and sacrificed, preached and prophesied, with a soul full of the purest aspirations, most unselfish purposes, and desires for a life devoted to God and man, too high and tender to bear the rough usage of this world.

It was a little remarkable that only one woman ever joined this community. Mrs. Lamb merely followed wheresoever her husband led, — "as ballast for his balloon," as she said, in her bright way.

Miss Jane Gage was a stout lady of mature years, sentimental, amiable, and lazy. She wrote verses copiously, and had vague yearnings and graspings after the unknown, which led her to believe herself fitted for a higher sphere than any she had yet adorned.

Having been a teacher, she was set to instructing the children in the common branches. Each adult member took a turn at the infants; and, as each taught in his own way, the result was a chronic state of chaos in the minds of these much-afflicted innocents.

Sleep, food, and poetic musings were the desires of dear Jane's life, and she shirked all duties as clogs upon her spirit's wings. Any thought of lending a hand with the domestic drudgery never occurred to her; and when to the question, "Are there any beasts of burden on the place?" Mrs. Lamb answered, with a face that told its own tale, "Only one woman!" the buxom Jane took no shame to herself, but laughed at the joke, and let the stout-hearted sister tug on alone.

Unfortunately, the poor lady hankered after the flesh-pots, and endeavored to stay herself with private sips of milk, crackers, and cheese, and on one dire occasion she partook of fish at a neighbor's table.

One of the children reported this sad lapse from virtue, and poor Jane was publicly reprimanded by Timon.

"I only took a little bit of the tail," sobbed the penitent poetess.

"Yes, but the whole fish had to be tortured and slain that you might tempt your carnal appetite with that one taste of the tail. Know ye not, consumers of flesh meat, that ye are nourishing the wolf and tiger in your bosoms?"

At this awful question and the peal of laughter which arose from some of the younger brethren, tickled by the ludicrous contrast between the stout sinner, the stern judge, and the naughty satisfaction of the young detective, poor Jane fled from the room to pack her trunk and return to the world where fishes' tails were not forbidden fruit.

Transcendental wild oats were sown broadcast that year, and the fame thereof has not yet ceased in the land; for, futile as this crop seemed to outsiders, it bore an invisible harvest, worth much to those who planted in earnest. As none of the members of this particular community have ever recounted their experiences before, a few of them may not be amiss, since the interest in these attempts has never died out and Fruitlands was the most ideal of all these castles in Spain.

A new dress was invented, since cotton, silk, and wool were forbidden as the product of slave-labor, worm-slaughter, and sheep-robbery. Tunics and trousers of brown linen were the only wear. The women's skirts were longer, and their straw hat-brims wider than the men's, and this was the only difference. Some persecution lent a charm to the costume, and the long-haired, linen-clad reformers quite enjoyed the mild martyrdom they endured when they left home.

Money was abjured, as the root of all evil. The produce of the land was to supply most of their wants, or be exchanged for the few things they could not grow. This idea had its inconveniences; but self-denial was the fashion, and it was surprising how many things one can do without. When they desired to travel, they walked, if possible, begged the loan of a vehicle, or boldly entered car or coach, and, stating their principles to the officials, took the consequences. Usually their dress, their earnest frankness, and gentle resolution won them a passage; but now and then they met with hard usage, and had the satisfaction of suffering for their principles.

On one of these penniless pilgrimages they took passage on a boat, and, when fare was demanded, artlessly offered to talk, instead of pay. As the boat was well under way and they actually had not a cent, there was no help for it. So Brothers Lion and Lamb held forth to the assembled passengers in their most eloquent style. There must have been something effective in this conversation, for the listeners were moved to take up a contribution for these inspired lunatics, who preached peace on earth and good-will to man so earnestly, with empty pockets. A goodly sum was collected; but when the captain presented it the reformers proved that they were consistent even in their madness, for not a penny would they accept, saying, with a look at the group about them, whose indifference or contempt had changed to interest and respect, "You see how well we get on without money"; and so went serenely on their way, with their linen blouses flapping airily in the cold October wind.

They preached vegetarianism everywhere and resisted all temptations of the flesh, contentedly eating apples and bread at well-spread tables, and much afflicting hospitable hostesses by denouncing their food and taking away their appetites, discussing the "horrors of shambles," the "incorporation of the brute in man," and "on elegant abstinence the sign of a pure soul." But, when the perplexed or offended ladies asked what they should eat, they got in reply a bill of fare consisting of "bowls of sunrise for breakfast," "solar seeds of the sphere," "dishes from Plutarch's chaste table," and other viands equally hard to find in any modern market.

Reform conventions of all sorts were haunted by these brethren, who said many wise things and did many foolish ones. Unfortunately, these wanderings interfered with their harvest at home; but the rule was to do what the spirit moved, so they left their crops to Providence and went a-reaping in wider and, let us hope, more fruitful fields than their own.

Luckily, the earthly providence who watched over Abel Lamb was at hand to glean the scanty crop yielded by the "uncorrupted land," which, "consecrated to human freedom," had received "the sober culture of devout men."

About the time the grain was ready to house, some call of the Oversoul wafted all the men away. An easterly storm was coming up and the yellow stacks were sure to be ruined. Then Sister Hope gathered her forces. Three little girls, one boy (Timon's son), and herself, harnessed to clothes-baskets and Russia-linen sheets, were the only teams she could command; but with these poor appliances the indomitable woman got in the grain and saved food for her young, with the instinct and energy of a mother-bird with a brood of hungry nestlings to feed.

This attempt at regeneration had its tragic as well as comic side, though the world only saw the former.

With the first frosts, the butterflies, who had sunned themselves in the new light through the summer, took flight, leaving the few bees to see what honey they had stored for winter use. Precious little appeared beyond the satisfaction of a few months of holy living.

At first it seemed as if a chance to try holy dying also was to be offered them. Timon, much disgusted with the failure of the scheme, decided to retire to the Shakers, who seemed to be the only successful community going.

"What is to become of us?" asked Mrs. Hope, for Abel was heart-broken at the bursting of his lovely bubble.

"You can stay here, if you like, till a tenant is found. No more wood must be cut, however, and no more corn ground. All I have must be sold to pay the debts of the concern, as the responsibility rests with me," was the cheering reply.

"Who is to pay us for what we have lost? I gave all I had, — furniture, time, strength, six months of my children's lives, — and all are wasted. Abel gave himself body and soul, and is almost wrecked by hard work and disappointment. Are we to have no return for this, but leave to starve and freeze in an old house, with winter at hand, no money, and hardly a friend left; for this wild scheme has alienated nearly all we had. You talk much about justice. Let us have a little, since there is nothing else left."

But the woman's appeal met with no reply but the old one: "It was an experiment. We all risked something, and must bear our losses as we can."

With this cold comfort, Timon departed with his son, and was absorbed into the Shaker brotherhood, where he soon found the order of things reversed, and it was all work and no play.

Then the tragedy began for the forsaken little family. Desolation and despair fell upon Abel. As his wife said, his new beliefs had alienated many friends. Some thought him mad, some unprincipled. Even the most kindly thought him a visionary, whom it was useless to help till he took more practical views of life. All stood aloof, saying: "Let him work out his own ideas, and see what they are worth."

He had tried, but it was a failure. The world was not ready for Utopia yet, and those who attempted to found it only got laughed at for their pains. In other days, men could sell all and give to the poor, lead lives devoted to holiness and high thought, and, after the persecution was over, find themselves honored as saints or martyrs. But in modern times these things are out of fashion. To live for one's principles, at all costs, is a dangerous speculation; and the failure of an ideal, no matter how humane and noble, is harder for the world to forgive and forget than bank robbery or the grand swindles of corrupt politicians.

Deep waters now for Abel, and for a time there seemed no passage through. Strength and spirits were exhausted by hard work and too much thought. Courage failed when, looking about for help, he saw no sympathizing face, no hand outstretched to help him, no voice to say cheerily,

"We all make mistakes, and it takes many experiences to shape a life. Try again, and let us help you."

Every door was closed, every eye averted, every heart cold, and no way open whereby he might earn bread for his children. His principles would not permit him to do many things that others did; and in the few fields where conscience would allow him to work, who would employ a man who had flown in the face of society, as he had done?

Then this dreamer, whose dream was the life of his life, resolved to carry out his idea to the bitter end. There seemed no place for him here, — no work, no friend. To go begging conditions was as ignoble as to go begging money. Better perish of want than sell one's soul for the sustenance of his body. Silently he lay down upon his bed, turned his face to the wall, and waited with pathetic patience for death to cut the knot which he could not untie. Days and nights went by, and neither food nor water passed his lips. Soul and body were dumbly struggling together, and no word of complaint betrayed what either suffered.

His wife, when tears and prayers were unavailing, sat down to wait the end with a mysterious awe and submission; for in this entire resignation of all things there was an eloquent significance to her who knew him as no other human being did.

"Leave all to God," was his belief; and in this crisis the loving soul clung to this faith, sure that the Allwise Father would not desert this child who tried to live so near to Him. Gathering her children about her, she waited the issue of the tragedy that was being enacted in that solitary room, while the first snow fell outside, untrodden by the footprints of a single friend.

But the strong angels who sustain and teach perplexed and troubled souls came and went, leaving no trace without, but working miracles within. For, when all other sentiments had faded into dimness, all other hopes died utterly; when the bitterness of death was nearly over, when body was past any pang of hunger or thirst, and soul stood ready to depart, the love that outlives all else refused to die. Head had bowed to defeat, hand had grown weary with too heavy tasks, but heart could not grow cold to those who lived in its tender depths, even when death touched it.

"My faithful wife, my little girls, — they have not forsaken me, they are mine by ties that none can break. What right have I to leave them alone? What right to escape from the burden and the sorrow I have helped to bring? This duty remains to me, and I must do it manfully. For their sakes, the world will forgive me in time; for their sakes, God will sustain me now."

Too feeble to rise, Abel groped for the food that always lay within his reach, and in the darkness and solitude of that memorable night ate and drank what was to him the bread and wine of a new communion, a new dedication of heart and life to the duties that were left him when the dreams fled.

In the early dawn, when that sad wife crept fearfully to see what change had come to the patient face on the pillow, she found it smiling at her, saw a wasted hand outstretched to her, and heard a feeble voice cry bravely, "Hope!"

What passed in that little room is not to be recorded except in the hearts of those who suffered and endured much for love's sake. Enough for us to know that soon the wan shadow of a man came forth, leaning on the arm that never failed him, to be welcomed and cherished by the children, who never forgot the experiences of that time.

"Hope" was the watchword now; and, while the last logs blazed on the hearth, the last bread and apples covered the table, the new commander, with recovered courage, said to her husband, —

"Leave all to God — and me. He has done his part, now I will do mine."

"But we have no money, dear."

"Yes, we have. I sold all we could spare, and have enough to take us away from this snowbank."

"Where can we go?"

"I have engaged four rooms at our good neighbor, Lovejoy's. There we can live cheaply till spring. Then for new plans and a home of our own, please God."

"But, Hope, your little store won't last long, and we have no friends."

"I can sew and you can chop wood. Lovejoy offers you the same pay as he gives his other men; my old friend, Mrs. Truman, will send me all the work I want; and my blessed brother stands by us to the end. Cheer up, dear heart, for while there is work and love in the world we shall not suffer."

"And while I have my good angel Hope, I shall not despair, even if I wait another thirty years before I step beyond the circle of the sacred little world in which I still have a place to fill."

So one bleak December day, with their few possessions piled on an ox-sled, the rosy children perched atop, and the parents trudging arm in arm behind, the exiles left their Eden and faced the world again.

"Ah, me! my happy dream. How much I leave behind that never can be mine again," said Abel, looking back at the lost Paradise, lying white and chill in its shroud of snow.

"Yes, dear; but how much we bring away," answered brave-hearted Hope, glancing from husband to children.

"Poor Fruitlands! The name was as great a failure as the rest!" continued Abel, with a sigh, as a frostbitten apple fell from a leafless bough at his feet.

But the sigh changed to a smile as his wife added, in a half-tender, half-satirical tone, —

"Don't you think Apple Slump would be a better name for it, dear?"

Suggestions for Additional Reading

On the historical background of the period 1820–1850, see John D. Hicks, *The Federal Union* (Boston, 1937), especially Chapter 25; or Carl R. Fish, *The Rise of the Common Man* (New York, 1927), one of the few attempts at a social history. The most recent and sympathetic account of Jacksonian Democracy and its ramifications is Arthur M. Schlesinger, Jr., *The Age of Jackson* (Boston, 1945). The industrial changes of the period are conveniently summarized in the first four chapters of Thomas C. Cochran and William Miller, *The Age of Enterprise* (New York, 1942). Part III of Chester W. Wright, *Economic History of the United States* (New York, 1941), provides a more systematic and detailed, though less lively, account of the economic developments.

There is no one adequate treatment of the transcendental movement as a whole. Van Wyck Brooks, *The Flowering of New England* (New York, 1936), gives vivid sketches of the important members of the group in their local habitations. On the philosophical side the best analyses are Harold C. Goddard, *Studies in New England Transcendentalism* (New York, 1908); Henry D. Gray, *Emerson: A Statement of New England Transcendentalism as Expressed in the Philosophy of Its Chief Exponent* (Stanford, Cal., 1917); George Santayana, "The Genteel Tradition in American Philosophy," in *Winds of Doctrine* (New York, 1913).

Individual transcendentalists have expressed their attitudes toward politics, reform movements, and commercial enterprise with some vigor. See Emerson's essays on "Politics" and "New England Reformers" in *Essays: Second Series* (1844); "Historic Notes on Life and Letters in New England" and "Chardon Street Convention" in *Lectures and Biographical Sketches* (1883). This material and more is conveniently collected in *The Portable Emerson* (Viking Press, 1946) with a valuable introduction by Mark Van Doren. Thoreau's *Walden* (1854) is a central document of transcendental opinion and should be read entire, with special emphasis on Chapters 1 and 2. From Thoreau's *Miscellanies* see "Paradise (to Be) Regained" (1843) and "Life without Principle" (1863).

Special studies that bear on this aspect of the subject are: Raymer McQuiston, *The Relation of Ralph Waldo Emerson to Public Affairs* (Lawrence, Kansas, 1923); Mildred Silver, "Emerson and the Idea of Progress," *American Literature*, 12 (1940), 1–19; Alexander C. Kern, "Emerson and Economics," *New England Quarterly*, 13 (1940), 678–696; Joseph W. Beach, "Emerson and Revolution," *University of Toronto Quarterly*, 3 (1934), 474–497; Arthur I. Ladu, "The Political Ideas of Theodore Parker," *Studies in Philology*, 33 (1941), 106–123.

Acquaintance with individual transcendentalists as persons may best be begun by consulting their journals: *The Heart of Emerson's Journals*, edited by Bliss Perry (Boston, 1926); *The Heart of Thoreau's Journals*, edited by Odell

Shepard (Boston, 1927); *The Journals of Bronson Alcott,* edited by Odell Shepard (Boston, 1938). From among many biographical and critical studies the following may be especially recommended: Bliss Perry, *Emerson Today* (Princeton, 1931), a brief book but filled with insight; Joseph W. Krutch, *Thoreau* (American Men of Letters, New York, 1948), an exceptionally lucid analysis of transcendental thinking; Odell Shepard, *Pedlar's Progress* (Boston, 1937), a full and scholarly tracing of the career of Bronson Alcott; Henry S. Commager, *Theodore Parker, Yankee Crusader* (Boston, 1936), a tribute to a Christian hero; and Octavius B. Frothingham, *George Ripley* (Boston, 1882), the only biography of a lesser figure.

Utopian movements in America are surveyed in Frances T. Russell, *Touring Utopia: The Realm of Constructive Humanism* (New York, 1932), or more popularly in Victor F. Calverton, *Where Angels Dared to Tread* (New York, 1941). On Brook Farm in particular, consult Katherine Burton, *Paradise Planters: The Story of Brook Farm* (New York, 1939); Lindsay Swift, *Brook Farm: Its Members, Scholars, and Visitors* (New York, 1900), encyclopedic and a trifle dull; John T. Codman, *Brook Farm: Historic and Personal Memoirs* (Boston, 1894); and Elizabeth P. Peabody, *Last Evening with Allston, and Other Papers* (Boston, 1886). The one informative study of Fruitlands is by Clara E. Sears, *Bronson Alcott's Fruitlands* (Boston, 1915).

Full bibliographical lists of writings dealing with individual authors may be found in the bibliography attached to Spiller, Thorp, Johnson, and Canby, *Literary History of the United States* (New York, 1948).